# The Democratic Soldier:
# The Life of
# General Gustave P. Cluseret

# The Democratic Soldier:
# The Life of
# General Gustave P. Cluseret

By

William J. Phalen

Vij Books India Pvt Ltd

New Delhi (India)

Published by

**Vij Books India Pvt Ltd**
(Publishers, Distributors and Importers)
2/19, Ansari Road
Delhi – 110 002
Phones: 91-11-43596460, 91-11-47340674
Fax: 91-11-47340674
e-mail: vijbooks@rediffmail.com


Copyright © 2015, *William J. Phalen*


ISBN      : 978-93-84464-94-3 (Paperback)

ISBN      : 978-93-84464-95-0 (ebook)

# Table of Contents

# Introduction

Called "a Frenchman always in search of a revolution" by Edward L. Pierce, a biographer of Senator Charles Sumner, Gustave Paul Cluseret, managed during his long life to become involved as a military figure in France, Ireland, and Italy, while also taking part in the American Civil War. Additionally, he was imprisoned twice by the French and condemned to death by both the British and the French. Cluseret published four books, edited a newspaper in the United States and contributed articles to newspapers and journals in Europe and the United States. He was an accomplished painter, and served as a spy for Senator Charles Sumner in Mexico and Europe. And finally near the end of his life he served in the French Chamber of Deputies.

In his obituary, the New York *Times* said of him that he was "of a treacherous character, unreliable and frequently connected with questionable enterprises which got him into trouble every where he went." He was also referred to as a Condottieri, a mercenary or sometimes simply as a soldier of fortune. While he had problems with authority, especially the incompetent kind, and was always an outrageous self-promoter, he genuinely supported the cause of freedom prompting him to join in civil wars in America and Europe.

# THE UNITED STATES

In 1861, Abraham Lincoln began calling for volunteers to support the Union cause. Secretary of State William Seward believed that it was the public interest to bring foreigners, "friends of freedom and the unity of the American Republic," into the armed forces.[1] Satisfactory positions had been assigned to all who offered, but the army was rapidly filling up. The United States had no dire need to offer special inducements beyond the compensation prescribed by the laws of Congress. As an example, the Department of the Army could not authorize George P. Marsh, the American ambassador to Italy to advance money to defray the expenses of volunteers from that country, although those who came would be accepted. But when self-appointed "generals" began to clutter departmental desks with applications, the official attitude slowly became less generous. By October 1861, Seward was writing that competition for commissioned officers would soon be so great as to leave latecomers unrewarded. Officers would be carefully screened for experience, good character, and conduct. Those who came soon might reasonably expect employment; those who should delay would probably find the armies filled, and Seward hoped, "the great battle won."[2] Seward's pronouncement reached one of the most hopeful aspirants, Gustave-Paul Cluseret, considering this to be a better opportunity than his service in Italy, Cluseret, a brigadier-general in the forces of Gussepi Garibaldi, marshaled his arguments for the attainment of a superior rank in the Union Army of the United States and began by importuning George P. Marsh, the American ambassador to Italy[3] to this end.

With Ambassador Marsh's support, Cluseret arrived in the United States in 1862 armed with letters of introduction from Garibaldi and such leading

---

1   Seward to Marsh, no.19, September 21, 1861, Washington, *Instructions – Italy*, vol.10

2   Seward to Marsh, no. 25, October 10, 1861, Washington, ibid.

3   Ella Lonn, *Foreigners in the Union Army and Navy* (Baton Rouge: Louisiana State University Press, 1951) p. 273-275

bourgeois republicans as Henri Martin, Emile Girardin, and Karl Blind. The support of these republicans was extremely important because in addition to the fact that Cluseret was closely associated with them, they were also highly regarded by the Senate Armed Services Committee, who looked upon them as "our friends" in Europe and anyone recommended by them was likely to receive special consideration at the hands of its' chairman, Elihu B. Washburne.[4] Fortunately for him, Cluseret also gained the attention of Senator Charles Sumner of Massachusetts, chairman of the Foreign Relations Committee. A relationship formed between Sumner and Cluseret that resulted in the sending of 116 letters from Cluseret to Sumner from 1861 to 1873 that are preserved among Sumner's papers.

Because of these connections, Cluseret was offered a position on the staff of Major General George B. McClellan, as aide-de-camp with the rank of colonel, he accepted and the promotion was made effective on March 10, 1862. This placement was not acceptable to McClellan however as he noted in his biography:

> Cluseret-afterwards Minister of War under the Commune-brought me a letter of introduction from Garibaldi, recommending him in the highest terms as a soldier, man of honor, etc. I did not like his appearance and declined his services; but without my knowledge or consent Stanton appointed him a Colonel on my staff. I still declined to have anything to do with him, and he was sent to the Mountain Department [commanded by Major General John C. Fremont], as chief of staff, I think.[5]

In writing his autobiography, McClellan obviously forgot that a month before Cluseret officially joined his staff; he wrote a letter to Seward describing Cluseret in favorable terms.

---

4    Elihu B. Wasburne, *Reflections of a Minister to France, 1869-1877* (New York: C. Scribner's Sons, 1887) p. 107

5    George B. McClellan, *McClellan's Own Story: The War For the Union, The Soldiers who Fought It, The Civilians who Directed It, and His Relations To It and To Them* (New York: Charles Webster and Company, 1887, p. 143

Hd Qtrs of the Army
Wash Feby 11 1861 [1862]

To

William H Seward
Hon WH Seward
Secty of State

Dear Sir:

I had an interview with Col. Cluseret, late of the Italian Army, introduced to me by Capt Mohain of the Suite of Prince de Joinville. Col C also brought me a letter of introduction from General Garibaldi. Col C whose "etat de service" is good informs me that he resigned his commission in the Italian army upon the insistence of Mr. Marsh, who had corresponded with the late Secty of War and yourself upon the subject. That he resigned after receiving what he regarded as a promise that he should have the grade of general of Brigade in our service.

He seems to be a gentleman and good soldier. He has been waiting here many weeks so that his slender means have been exhausted. May I ask you to inform me whether your records throw any light on the case and whether the good faith of the Govt is pledged to this officer?

The Sect of War being absent from his office it seemed better to address you direct without delay as Col C has been waiting a long time.

Very truly and respectfully

Geo. B. McClellan

Maj Genl Comdg USA[6][7]

---

6   Stephen W. Sears, *The Civil War Papers of George B. McClellan: Selected Correspondence, 1860-1865* (Cambridge: Da Capo Press, 1992) p. 176

7   Seward replied the next day that in order to conciliate European opinion it would be "good policy" to accommodate Cluseret. ALS, Seward Papers, Rush Rheen Library, University of Rochester.

By the summer of 1862 Cluseret began looking for something better than a staff position with McClellan, as a professional soldier, soldiering was in his blood and the Frenchman took extraordinary pride in his martial skills. As he explained to Sumner, "I have a military reputation to preserve, [for] I have studied much and experienced much, [and] I am known in France and Italy as an up-and-coming officer."[8] At first, his prospects in America looked just as good. He had joined McClellan's staff and this combined with his recommendations from Europe and the contacts that he had established with Sumner, Seward, and the Secretary of War should have given him what he wanted, a commission as a brigadier general, a rank he deemed commensurate with his past experiences and his ties to French republicanism.

Fortunately, Cluseret was sent to John C. Fremont's command in the Mountain Department of western Virginia by Senator Sumner who believed that the Pathfinder's[9] Radical Republicanism would be more in line with Cluseret's political tastes than the more conservative McClellan.[10] This posting became an opportunity for Cluseret since although Fremont joined the American military in 1838, most of his experience had been in exploration rather than fighting. President Lincoln had tendered him a commission as a major general in May of 1861 due to his political reputation and influence. Whatever benefits the president hoped to derive from the appointment nearly disappeared altogether that August when Fremont imposed martial law in Missouri and declared free slaves who belonged to any secessionist. Coming at a time when Lincoln was anxious about the allegiance of the Border States, the proclamation portended disaster on both the military and political fronts. After Fremont refused Lincoln's request to modify the proclamation, the president ordered that the section in question be struck. Later Cluseret would also have a problem with a superior over civilians. At this time however, Cluseret, still a Colonel, was made aide-de-camp to Fremont, given the 8th West Virginia Infantry and the 60th Ohio Infantry, and placed in charge of Fremont's advance guard. In this position, two of his character traits emerged that would eventually lead to his advancement on the one hand and his loss

---

8     Cluseret to Sumner, August 19, 1862

9     This nickname was given John Fremont because of his explorations in the Western United States.

10    Gustave P. Cluseret, *Memories* (Paris: 1887) p. 81

of his command on the other. The first was his foreignness that was probably responsible for a lack of communication between Cluseret and his officers leading to a breakdown of discipline and morale in his unit (although it should be noted that both the 8th West Virginia and the 60th Ohio were new regiments that had just been recruited and sent to Fremont). This situation would be repeated when he was under the command of General Robert H. Milroy. The second was his assertiveness; given the opportunity to use his skills and because Fremont's forte was not military organization and who failed to delineate properly the advance guard's role and position within his command, Cluseret proceeded as if the army were on the offensive. Pushing forward with his cavalry on June 1, in disregard of orders to hold back, he ascertained that Stonewall Jackson's army, contrary to the impression at headquarters, was actually in retreat. Unfortunately, his dispatch, written in French arrived too late to be acted upon.[11] The following is an account of the actions of Cluseret's unit that evening as seen by Major and Brevet Colonel Theodore F. Lang of the 6th West Virginia Cavalry.

A reconnaissance by Colonel Cluseret with the 8th West Virginia and 60th Ohio pushed rapidly towards Strasburg [Virginia], when within a short distance of the town he learned that the enemy had vacated the place. So, with the addition of a battalion of cavalry and a section of artillery, he was ordered to take possession of the town. Night brought with it one of those terrible storms that had become so frequent of late, and this one excelled in its downpour of rain, and the lightning and thunder were indescribable. It was simply terrifically grand.

A thrilling incident, in which Colonel Cluseret and his command were the actors, is worthy of mention. The night just referred to was simply black in its darkness, and but for the vivid flash of the lightning for the moment one could not see his outstretched hand. Colonel Cluseret, being without guides and unfamiliar with the country, passed through the town, which was in darkness, and marching on saw lights in the distance, which he supposed was the town, but upon approaching the same, about 11 o'clock, the lights proved to be the enemies campfires, and he found himself in the midst of Ashby's[12]

---

11  Lowell L. Blaisdell, "A French Civil War Adventurer: Fact and Fancy," *Civil War History*, Vol. XIII, September 1966, No. III, p. 247-248

12  Brigadier General Turner Ashby, Stonewall Jacksons' cavalry commander

cavalry, which was the rear-guard of Jackson's army. Colonel Cluseret at once gave the order to charge, but at the sharp fire of Ashby's men the cavalry broke in a shameful panic, carrying back with it the artillery. To the honor and praise of the 8th West Virginia and 60th Ohio, not a man of them followed the disgraceful example, but stood their ground like veterans, and delivered such a steady and well-directed fire that the movement of Ashby was checked.

Colonel Cluseret, having accomplished the objectives of his reconnaissance, withdrew his men and returned to the main column...this battle in the dark was [Cluseret's regiment's] first introduction to powder and bullet at the hands of the enemy; they were, therefore, the more to be praised for their gallantry.[13]

On June 2 Fremont's army was again in motion, and now realizing that Jackson was retreating, closely pursued the Confederates. As before, Cluseret's units were in the van, continuously following and engaging the enemy's rear. In one of Fremont's engagements with Jackson, Union Brigadier General George D. Bayard was ambushed in a wooded area southeast of Harrisonburg, Virginia

At the critical moment in this episode, Colonel Cluseret, with his brigade, came to the relief [of] General Bayard, when the enemy retreated in disorder, leaving our forces in possession of their camp, with their dead and wounded left in our hands.[14]

For days several from this point on, Jackson continued to retreat, harassed by Fremont. On June 8th the Battle of Cross Keys took place, Major Lang –

About 8 a.m. heavy musketry firing was heard in our front, indicating that Colonel Cluseret [now commanding the 39th New York (the Garibaldi Guards) as well as the 8th Virginia and the 60th Ohio] was engaging the enemy. The effect of this firing accelerated the step of the whole command, and we soon learned that the enemy had placed a regiment – the 15th Alabama, Colonel Cantey- as outpost at Union Church, and it was this force that

---

13    Theodore F. Land, *Loyal West Virginia, From 1861 to 1865* (Baltimore, Maryland: The Deutsch Publishing Co., 1865) p. 76

14    Ibid. p. 79

Cluseret was engaging.

The enemy stubbornly fell back through the timber at a distance of a mile or more, Cluseret vigorously advancing. At this point Jackson's main force was found in the line of battle, which was naturally a strong one, and selected at leisure on the preceding day, which gave to Jackson a great advantage over General Fremont; but this is one of the inevitable conditions in war, and General Fremont had no choice but to go in and make the best of it.

The placing of his command in line of battle was regarded by all as especially skillful, and was about in the following order: Colonel Cluseret's brigade, which had pushed the forces opposed to it back upon the enemy's main line, held their position, which was well to the front and near the center.[15]

In the Cross Keys engagement, Cluseret performed very energetically, and possibly insubordinately. Early in the battle after striking the Confederate left-center, he apparently ignored orders to pull back into line with the rest of Fremont's command, instead holding the forward position for many hours despite repeated counter-attacks.[16] Cluseret sensed, as did other high-ranking officers, that a vigorous offensive would very likely dislodge the southerners.[17] Fremont's timidity during and immediately after the battle of Cross Keys was incomprehensible to Cluseret and puzzling to other high-ranking officers. In later years he labeled Fremont an incompetent for his mishandling of the battle of Cross Keys.

Cluseret's poor opinion of Fremont did not extend to the Union soldiers, whose performance during the Cross Keys engagement left an indelible impression on him. Drawing a subsequent comparison between regular troops trained in Europe with his command in the Union army, he declared:

I have served in many armies, I have seem armies put to rough tests under difficult climates, but never have I seen troops submitted to as adverse conditions as those of Fremont's army in the Shenandoah in 1862: They

---

15    Ibid. p. 82

16    Cluseret, Memories, p.82-83

17    Ibid, p.82-83

lacked cover, food, were faced with torrential rains…yet marched and fought equally day and night. The discipline and training of the barracks would never have inculcated in regular troops the feeling of abnegation and the strength of resistance that the Virginia mountaineers displayed in their love of liberty and country.[18]

Because of Cluseret's actions at Cross Keys, Fremont sent the following message to Stanton :

Headquarters Mountain Department
Harrisonburgh, Va., June 9

Hon. E. M. Stanton, Secretary of War:

In my dispatch of yesterday I omitted to state that Col. Cluseret's brigade, consisting of the Sixtieth Ohio and Eight [West] Virginia, afterward supported by the Garibaldi Guard, formed our advance and commenced the battle of Cross Keys, by sharp skirmishing, at nine o'clock in the morning. During the day they obtained possession of the enemies ground, which was disputed foot by foot, and only withdrew at evening when ordered to retire to a suitable position for the night.

The skill and gallantry displayed by Cluseret on this and frequent former occasions during the pursuit in which we have been engaged deserve high praise.

Respectfully,

J.C. Fremont,
Major-General[19]

Due to support such as the above coupled with his own self promoting efforts, as in a letter that he sent to President Lincoln informing him that "as the grandson of one by the side of Lafayette nearly a century ago fought for the stars and stripes," he felt rightly entitled to a brigadier generalship.[20] The

---

18   Gustave Cluseret, *Armee et democratie* (Paris, 1869) p. 20

19   Frank Moore, *The Rebellion Record: A Diary of American Events, with Documents, Narratives, Illustrative Incidents, Poetry, Etc.* (New York: G.P. Putnam, 1868) p. 105

20   Cluseret to Lincoln, April 7, 1862 (Headquarters of the Union Army, Department of the

promotion was given to him by Fremont, and supported by Lincoln, through a personal appeal by Sumner in which he described Cluseret as a "gallant Frenchman."[21]The promotion came on October 14, 1862, however it was not permanent because it lacked senatorial conformation, a prerequisite for this rank.[22]

In June of 1862, the Union army underwent a major command change. A new army group entitled The Army of Virginia was created under the command of Major General John Pope, which would include Fremont's forces. General Fremont stood the Second Major General on the list of the Regular Army – ranked only by McClellan. This change could take place because of a law passed during the previous April providing that the President might, at his discretion, assign in the field, the command of forces, "without regard to seniority of rank" as between any two officers present, of the "same grade." Allowing Pope, the junior, to supersede Fremont, the senior. Fremont believing that he was superior to Pope retired. [23]

Cluseret was put under the command of Brigadier General Robert H. Milroy, with whom he had fought at the Battle of Cross Keys. While Pope was as incompetent as Fremont, Milroy was an experienced military leader who had a penchant for fighting and loved combat as much as Cluseret. Both were ambitious, and they both wrote a copious amount of letters to those who could be of service to them. Most of Cluseret's letters went to Senator Charles Sumner, Milroy's to Republican Congressman Schuyler Colfax of Indiana, Speaker of the House of Representatives, trying to convince him to speak with General McClellan to see if "Little Mac" might be able to find Milroy a better command, one in which he could see more action.[24]

---

Army, National Archives)

21   Elihu B. Washburne, p. 107

22   The promotion was also supported by Major General Franz Sigel, who in a letter to Stanton, highly recommended Col. Cluseret and asked that he "be placed in command of a brigade and if possible be assigned to the 1st Corps, Army of Virginia. Letter for sale in the possession of Ira and Larry Goldberg Coins and Collectibles, Inc.

23   The resignation of Fremont affected Cluseret after he also resigned from the United States military and initially supported Fremont's bid for the presidency in 1864 by editing a newspaper, *The Nation*, which backed Fremont's candidacy.

24   Jonathan A. Noyalas, *My Will is Absolute Law, A Biography of Union General Robert H. Milroy* (Jefferson, North Carolina: McFarland and Company, Publishers, 2006) p. 32

At first Milroy was a supporter of Cluseret, writing to Brigadier General Jacob Dolson Cox after the Battle of Cross Keys, Milroy said of Cluseret

General Cluseret is forty years of age; was general of a French military school in which he afterwards taught for several years; served fourteen years in the French army, ten in Algiers and through the Crimean War; received the star of the Legion of Honor for distinguished service in the French revolution of 1848, and a badge of honor for distinguished service at Sebastopol; served through the campaigns of Fremont and Siegel as Colonel, and was made a Brigadier General for his gallantry at Cross Keys. Being an ardent admirer of our government and having come to fight for its existence, and being a gentleman of fine intellect and splendid military knowledge, I think his opinion worthy of consideration[25]

This high opinion of Cluseret on the part of Milroy continued through the fall and winter of 1862, and then changed. According to Cox:

Milroy was for a time loud in his praises of Cluseret as the *beau ideal* of an officer, and their friendship was fraternal. In the winter, however, their mutual admiration was nipped by a killing frost, and a controversy sprung up between them which soon led to mutual recrimination also in the superlative degree. They addressed their complaints to General Halleck, and as the papers passed through my headquarters, I was a witness of their berating of each other, but I cannot recall anything very serious in their accusations.[26]

Referring to this incident, Cox said in his memoirs, "An amusing interlude occurred in a hot controversy which arose between General Milroy and one of his subordinates which would not be worth mentioning except for the fact that the subordinate (Cluseret) had afterward a world-wide notoriety as military chief of the Paris Commune in 1870"[27]

The controversy between Cluseret and Milroy was far from amusing however since it had to do with the treatment of Confederate non-combatants.

---

25   Cornelia McDonald, A Diary, with Reminiscences of the War and Refugee Life in the Shenandoah Valley 1860-1865 (Louisville: Cullom and Ghertner, 1935) p. 121

26   Jacob D. Cox, *Military Reminiscences of the Civil War, Volume 1, April 1861-November 1863* (New York: Charles Scribner's Sons, 1900) p. 427

27   Ibid. p. 426

Cluseret believed lenient treatment to be the best means of gaining support of the civilian citizens in an area (Winchester, Virginia)[28] that had repeatedly changed hands. Therefore he went out of his way to accommodate the pro-Confederate population, while imposing rigid discipline on his soldiers. When Milroy, an ardent abolitionist joined Cluseret at Winchester, he reversed Cluseret's policy, thereby affronting his dignity.[29] Milroy's attitude toward Confederate civilians is illustrated in a letter to his wife after establishing martial law in Winchester, "I can now realize something of the weighty and unpleasant responsibility that rests on a king...my will is absolute law – none dare contradict or dispute my slightest word or wish...both male and female tremble when they come into my presence...I feel a strong disposition to play the tyrant among these traitors."[30]

Aside from his problems with Milroy, Cluseret also brought upon himself problems with the high command over the use of his pen and the potential use of his sword. At this time (late December, 1862), supreme headquarters had adopted a defensive position in the Shenandoah Valley. During the previous month, Cluseret had contacted Cox correctly predicting Jackson's moves in the Valley and suggesting that he and Milroy (Cluseret's superior) be permitted to attack the Confederate supply center at Staunton, Virginia. When the Staunton attack was rejected, Cluseret wrote to headquarters asking that his appointment to the rank of brigadier be immediately confirmed and when this request was rejected, wrote to Halleck asking that he be given an independent command in Texas. He also had difficulties with a fellow officer, Colonel Joseph Keifer over the treatment of a captured Confederate officer who had indulged in a minor guerrilla escapade. While Cluseret favored great leniency toward civilians, he urged summery execution in this case. Keifer won the argument because Lincoln absolutely forbade any officer from imposing such a penalty at this time on his on initiative.

Cluseret again wrote to Halleck asking to be relieved of further service in Milroy's command and also wrote to Secretary of State Seward a letter

---

28  Late in December 1862, Cluseret successfully recaptured the town.

29  Cluseret to Seward, January, 12,1863 (Hdqts. of the Union Army, Dept. of the Army, Nat. Archives)

30  Milroy to Mary Milroy, January 18, 1863, Robert H. Milroy collection, Jasper County Public Library, Rensselaer, Indiana.

airing his grievances. Milroy added the following to the letter to Halleck: "Most heartily approved and respectfully forwarded, I have been grossly deceived and humbugged by this foreigner, and recommend that he be not only relieved from service in my division, but also in the U.S. army, for the good of the service.[31]

During the previous November, supreme headquarters went through a process of reorganization; Lincoln replaced McCellan with Major General Ambrose Burnside. Burnside was at best a reluctant fighter, and this produced a distinct desire for a quiet, defensive position in the Shenandoah Valley[32]

Contrary to the plans of his commanders, Cluseret wrote to Major General Jacob Cox about an idea for an attack in the Shenandoah to force Stonewall Jackson into moving by threatening the Confederate rail and supply center at Staunton, Virginia:

Maj. Gen. Jacob D. Cox
New Creek,
November 19, 1862.
Received at Charleston, W. Va., November 20.

Gen.:

I do not think there is the least use of our remaining at New Creek. As we [Milroy and Cluseret] told Gen. Kelly, his fears were entirely without foundation. What interest can Jackson possibly have to destroy more of the railroad than he has done, when we reflect on the risk and possible consequences that may arise to him from pushing up into the north-west? The object of destroying a railroad is not so much to capture property as to destroy communication. The latter object has already attained; further destruction would not advance that object; it would be a piece of folly or deliberate malice, of neither of which Jackson is ever guilty. His position and the disposition of his forces clearly indicate a very different object. Posted on the right flank, and in the rear of the army of Burnside, behind passes by which he can debouch at will to a point between that army and the capital, he is in no standing danger, and can be dislodged from his position only by

---

31  Cluseret and Milroy to Halleck, January 9, 1863 (Hdqrs. of the Union Army, Dept. of the Army, Nat. Archives)

32  Lowell L. Blaisdell, "A French Civil War Adventurer: Fact and Fancy", p. 251

a battle or a strategic movement. It is absolutely impossible that he should forgo the advantages of such a position to move upon a foolish expedition, which no military man would ever conceive of. What use are we? He [General Kelly], then, absolutely knows that Jackson ought to be dislodged. There are naturally two means of doing this: one by attacking him, which will not probably be done, but which, had I the power, should by all means be done, by a corps detached on the east from Burnside's army and a combination of the troops of Harper's Ferry, Hagerstown, Cumberland, and New Creek from the west, got together in all speed, and by means of the railroad. The other means is by a strategic movement, which I shall point out. Threaten at once Staunton and the railroad of the South. Jackson will then do one of two things-either he will march through the valley to relieve the threatened point and rejoin the Southern army, in which case he will leave Winchester and the Baltimore and Ohio Railroad open, or he will remain where he is, and we can destroy a line of communication and a depot of supplies much more important than the dangers occasioned by his position at Winchester.

Now, Staunton and the railroad can be threatened as follows: First, by reuniting our whole force at Beverly; second, from that point to march upon Warm Springs and fall upon the troops there, or, according to circumstances, pass over to the east of that place and fall suddenly upon Staunton, and destroy the railroad bridges between that place and Charlottesville; but this is a plan that only can be matured on the spot; third a strong detachment of troops, under Gen. Cox, should make a demonstration against Lewisburg, threatening the railroad of the south.

In all probably, if the demonstration is well made, the rebels at Warm Springs will unite with those at Lewisburg, and we can profit rapidly of that movement by falling upon Staunton. If, on the contrary, the troops at Lewisburg are left to themselves, we can each move separately, as we are much stronger, and thus open a double way to Staunton and the railroad to the south. For the execution of the plan we need 1000 cavalry, or a full regiment, which must be had, if only temporarily.

Respectfully,

G.P. CLUSERET, Brig.-Gen.[33]

33  Letter reproduced from *The War of the Rebellion: Official Records of the Union and Confederate Armies*, Series 1, Volume 21, Serial No.31 (Broadfoot Publishing Company:

When Fremont resigned his command the previous July, it was arguably the nation's gain, but it was definitely Cluseret's loss, for he neither liked nor respected his new superiors. They were timid, he complained to civilian authorities, when they did not act on what he believed to be obvious as the plan he outlined to Cox. In his professional opinion, men like Cox and Kelly were "excellent lawyers no doubt,' but they made decisions that that were "the very reverse… [of those made by] a man used to *the trade.*" He wrote to Sumner, finally, that "it is impossible for me to ignore the radical nullity that surrounds me."

I can do nothing better than to compare [my superiors]…to a professor of rhetoric who comes to the theater to perform *Esther* or *Athalie* under the pretext of having studied Racine, [though] never having seen footlights or audiences, nor ever having trod the boards - - he would be the most grotesque character in the world. It is the same with these generals in the field of battle.[34]

Perhaps Cluseret's complaints were caused by the fact that ever since the battle of Cross Keys, he had not been involved in the main action. In early August, at the time of Jackson's moves leading to the battle of Cedar Mountain, the Frenchman, on a scouting mission, forwarded an accurate warning of the Confederate general's advance. However the message, amidst a host of others, made no impression on Major General John Pope, the commanding officer, who exceeded Fremont in incompetence. He had also asked for an independent command in Texas and had been turned down by Halleck.[35] Additionally, Halleck blocked Cluseret's transfer to the command of Major General William Rosecrans, warning him about Cluseret: "If you knew him better, you would not ask for him. You will regret the application as long as you live.[36]

The end of Cluseret's American military career came when Milroy induced his political friends in Indiana to insure that there would be no

---

Wilmington, NC, 1997) p. 779-780

34    Cluseret to Steward, December 29, 1862, Seward Papers, University of Rochester

35    Cluseret to Halleck, Nov. 29, 1862 (Hdqrs of the Union Army, Dept. of the Army, Nat. Archives).

36    Halleck to Rosecrans, Jan. 25, 1863 (*The War of the Rebellion: A Compilation of the Official Records of the Union and Confederate Armies*, Series 1, Vol. XXIII, Part II Correspondence, etc., Washington, 1889) P. 11-12

senatorial confirmation of Cluseret's brigadier general's commission. Further, even though Milroy never emphatically spelled out the reason for his problem with Cluseret, it was probably Cluseret's lack of enthusiasm for Milroy's policies. Writing to his superior, General Robert Schenck, Milroy said of Cluseret, "I have had trouble with Genl. Cluseret, I …observed that his harsh disrespectful and unfeeling course towards his officers and men, and the difficulty in their understanding him and him them, was making him very unpopular… [Cluseret is] hasty tempered impatient insulting tyrannical and overbearing to those under him."[37] The result was that while Milroy may have forced Cluseret to resign his command during the second week in January, Cluseret did not officially relinquish his commission until May of 1863. Driving people out of the service who did not support Lincoln's emancipation policy was not something unique to Milroy. Other federal officers including Gen. Ulysses S. Grant, dismissed subordinates who failed to see the advantages that emancipation presented to the Union war effort.[38]

Regardless of Milroy's animosity toward Cluseret, at least nine officers of Cluseret's brigade had problems with him. Two days after Milroy came to Winchester, officers from Cluseret's brigade respectfully requested "that the Gen. [Cluseret] now in command of the Brigade should be relieved." The officers complained that he was a "foreigner unable to speak our language so as to be understood and he himself has some difficulty in understanding us hence our intercourse thus far has been nothing but a perplexing series of mutual blunders and mistakes."[39] They protested further: "He has shown the utmost disregard and contempt for the rights and feelings of officers… below him in rank, repelling them with a tyrannical and despotic air when in the conscientious discharge of their duty to theirs commands they applied to him in a respectful manner for a redress of their grievances…he is to play the tyrant over all who belong to his command." The angry officers closed their letter to Milroy by informing him that Cluseret should be dismissed because he was simply not one of them, he was a European. He knows nothing of the genius of our institutions," the officers explained to Milroy, "or the spirit

---

37    Milroy to Schenck, January 17, 1863, Schenck Papers, University of Miami, Ohio

38    David W. Blight and Brooks D. Simpson, eds. *Union and Emancipation: Essays on Politics and Race in the Civil War Era* (Kent, Ohio: Kent State University Press, 1997) p. 125

39    Officers of Cluseret's brigade to Milroy, January 3, 1863, Robert H. Milroy's Papers, Japer County Public Library, Rensselair, Indiana

of our people and whilst he might do to command an army of European conscripts he can never command an army of American volunteers.[40] And a more specific charge by the Frenchman's officers during a skirmish with a small band of Confederate cavalry at Winchester, Virginia, "there was so much confusion in the disposition and in his own understanding of that disposition that we find him ordering infantry to fire on his Cavalry whereby one horse was killed and the lives of men put in jeopardy at the hands of their friends. [41] Complaints such as these about Cluseret's ability would become fuel for Milroy to rid himself of Cluseret. Whether he left the service of his own accord, or was pushed out by Milroy, it was a hard blow for him to take. Displaying his disgust to Seward at this time and referring to Halleck he wrote "…Disasters without number have befallen the public…since he came to power. It is impossible to come to a conclusion in regard to him otherwise than in one of two words *incapable* or *culpable* – I consider him as absolutely responsible for the failures of McClellan, Burnside, Pope, Banks, etc., etc." As an accomplished army officer in the French, Italian, and now the Union military, Cluseret had had enough of such amateur leadership.[42] , [43] Cluseret was right about these generals; he also thought he was doing his duty by reporting their faults to his patrons in Washington. Yet in the process, he only managed to alienate the military authorities and reinforce his growing reputation as a troublemaker.

While Cluseret was mainly responsible for the problems that he had with his military commanders, the real loser was not he, but, according to him, the United States. He explained this in a letter to Sumner written a year after his resignation that the real tragedy of his short American military career was the way it had traduced the traditional Franco-American commitment to democracy. "You know," he told the Massachusetts senator, "what motive convinced me to leave Europe and destroy my career in order to come to America":

---

40   Ibid.

41   Ibid.

42   Cluseret to Seward, May 1, 1863 (This letter was written after Cluseret had resigned from the army, since his name does not appear in the Army Register dated April 1, 1863)

43   Lincoln also thought little of Halleck, referring to him as "little more than a first rate clerk"

My intention in placing my sword in the service of the [Union] cause… was to rebuild democratically what Lafayette had once built in a completely different manner. I believe I can add, without too much vanity, that I was better versed in the ways of my craft than was the young marquis…[But the politics of the Union Army] presented me with the sad alternative of sacrificing my dignity, my duty, [and] my conscience…to my political ideals." [44]

In hindsight, he may have been right, but Lafayette had George Washington, Cluseret had George McClellan.

As much as Cluseret came to dislike American military commanders, he again wrote about his admiration for the average American soldier as he did after the Battle of Cross Keys, whose "conduct…surpassed all my expectations. "Everywhere he served the Union soldiers suffered gracefully under adverse conditions without complaining or requiring harsh discipline…something *unheard* of in Europe." The reason for this, concluded Cluseret, was that Yankee soldiers were citizens first and fighters second. [45]

"The soldier," he wrote in 1869, "must never cease to be a citizen; he must, on the contrary, take an active, direct part in the affairs of the country." American soldiers did take an active part, and Cluseret was amazed at the effort this sometimes involved:

If the American volunteers accomplished prodigies of patience, energy, and devotion at the commencement of the war, it is because they fought with knowledge of the cause. In the midst of the messiest business one could hear the squeaking voice of the *"news boy"* over the sound of the fusillade…The soldier… [bought his] newspaper, stuffing it under the flap of his pack; and at the first break, he ran his eyes quickly over it. After reading it, one could see his face light up or become somber. But whatever his feelings, there would be a redoubling of his zeal and drive. [46]

Cluseret thought this was a vivid example of an average American's fitness for self-government, or what might be called the "republican capacity." [47]

---

44   Cluseret to Sumner, March 1, 1864

45   Cluseret to Sumner, May 11, 1862

46   Gustave Paul Cluseret, *Armee et Democratie* p. 101-102

47   Philip Mark Katz, *Americanizing The Paris Commune*, 1861-1868 PhD. Dissertation,

One officer that Cluseret liked and admired (although not as a military commander) was Fremont, probably because he allowed Cluseret to fight, usually putting him in his advance guard. Fremont was not essentially an experienced military leader, but rather an explorer (hence the nickname, the Pathfinder) Lincoln tendered him a commission as a major general in May of 1861, and gave him command of the Army of the West (he was the first presidential candidate of the Republican Party). Two months later, Lincoln removed Fremont who subsequently obtained the command in the Shenandoah Valley, where he came into contact with Cluseret. After performing poorly, Fremont was again removed from command, court martialed, and then given a presidential pardon. All of which undoubtedly induced Fremont to again come to grips with Lincoln, this time as one of his opponents for the presidency in 1864.

This action on the part of Fremont provided Cluseret with the opportunity to exhibit his second career, journalism. To publicize his campaign, Fremont created a political journal, *The New Nation*. The journal was a logical development once Fremont decided to resume his political career in the early months of 1864. His first step was to rally old and new supporters to his cause. With his considerable personal wealth the task of establishing a newspaper to serve as his personal organ was not a major problem. To find an editor-in chief, Fremont looked into his entourage and selected one of his former field officers, Gustave-Paul Cluseret.

Fremont probably chose Cluseret, a professional soldier with a peripatetic career in the French, Italian, and Union armies because; first Fremont and his wife were well-known Francophiles, and second, Cluseret's background as a journalist when not engaged in military matters. At that time while in America, Cluseret had sent articles on the American Civil War, which had been published in such French journals as the *Siecle* and the *Revue Nationale* as well as also having some of his material printed in American newspapers such as the *Evening Post*. Next, by training and experience, Cluseret had to be regarded as an expert on military affairs. Since a good deal of the editorial thrust of *The New Nation* was to be concerned with the military conduct of the war, Cluseret with his background had good credentials. Finally, there was his politics. Since Cluseret had been a recent associate of Garibaldi and the cosmopolitan host of Republicans who had flocked to the Red shirt cause, and as a republican himself, it was natural that he sought out the Radical Republican element in America. It was probably his political convictions that got him assigned to Fremont after leaving McClellan's staff; it was certainly his political leanings that encouraged his friendship with Senator Charles Sumner of Massachusetts. If one can believe Cluseret, their friendship was an extremely close one, so close that it can lead to speculation as to whether or not Sumner played any role in encouraging Cluseret's eventual anti-Fremont stand. Cluseret accepted the position, even though he was personally committed to the promotion of Sumner's presidential ambitions.[48] Initially he and Fremont concealed the real purpose of the paper, representing it as merely an outspoken independent journal. At the same time, Cluseret concealed from Fremont that, in an attempt to pacify Sumner, he was assuring him that the entire move was simply a preparation for Sumner's ultimate candidacy for the Presidency in the 1868 elections, in accord with Sumner's own perspectives on the question.[49]

Ostensibly, Cluseret had two simple goals: to make the Pathfinder President and to make his own mark on New York journalism. According to the *New York Times,* Cluseret also brought a flair for the polemic to the task, as he proceeded to fill the pages of *The New Nation* with equal parts Fremont, vitriol, and "contemporary European ultra-democratic theories."[50]

Fremont's platform foreshadowed the major planks of Radical Republicanism, especially the expansion of Congressional authority and the parallel reduction of Executive power (especially when it came to patronage); the platform also called for a restructuring of the army, strong support for the Monroe Doctrine, and the creation of a truly "national spirit."[51] Cluseret also stressed a number of themes that were as much a part of his old life in French republican politics as his new life in America; the expansion of democratic participation, the end of French adventurism in Mexico, and the decentralization of authority.

---

48   Cluseret to Sumner, New York, March 31, 1864, Sumner Papers, Vol. 139

49   Ibid.

50   *The New York Times,* Sept. 12, 1872

51   These themes were laid out in the first issue of *The New Nation,* and constantly reiterated

The last point was probably the most important. Since well before Tocqueville, opposition parties in France had focused on centralization as the primary source of all political woes. Cluseret brought this same attitude to American politics in 1864, complaining to Sumner "[today] there is an America of Virginians, of Georgians, [and so on, but] not of Americans. [W]e must create a spirit of national unity, without falling into the [evils] of centralization." [52]

As editor of *The New Nation*, Cluseret launched the first edition in March 1864, he and his staff receiving a combined salary of $185.00 per week.[53] Theoretically, the editor was free to set his own policy, which came down to accomplishing one essential task; to make his readers aware of Fremont's presence as a public figure and to disassociate Fremont from the military and diplomatic failures plaguing the nation at this time. To accomplish this, Cluseret patterned his ideas at the time on contemporary European ultra-democratic theories, which advocated direct democracy and a one-term presidency. He envisioned a promising American future for himself as an *eminence grise*, first by backing Fremont as a win-the-war president, and secondly, as he wrote to Sumner, by backing the Bay Stater for the ensuing term as a Radical reconstructor.[54]

The beginning of Fremont's campaign took the form of a public meeting at Cooper Union on March 18, at which Horace Greeley spoke somewhat inconclusively in favor of Fremont.[55] As it seemed likely that the Republican nomination would go to Lincoln, the Fremonters expounded a strategy that was to be distinct from that envisioned by the professionally controlled regular Republicans who were to assemble in Baltimore; they not only called for grand popular assemblage, but, in addition, sought the support of the "War Democrats" as a means of broadening their voter's base.[56]

Cluseret began by publishing a series of military sketches. The first of these, serialized in three successive issues concerned General-in-Chief Henry

---

52   Cluseret to Sumner, late Feb., 1864

53   Explained in *The New Nation*, July 2, 1864

54   Ibid, March 31, 1864

55   *New York World*, March 19, 1864

56   *The New Nation*, March 12, 26; April 2, 16, 23; May 7,21; June 4, 1864

Halleck, an old California rival of Fremont. As edition succeeded edition, Halleck appeared not only as a man of mediocre ability but one whose actions early in the war appeared openly treasonous; Cluseret asserted that Halleck, with General Philip Kearney's support – another of Fremont's old rivals – had been engaged in a struggle to win California for the Confederacy, while Fremont had fought to keep it loyal to the union.[57] Just why a man with such a background should have been appointed to the key position of General-in-Chief was obvious. In Cluseret's words:

He was placed where he is in order to keep in the background all those whose military successes might give them strong claims to becoming candidates for the presidency.[58]

Thus Cluseret in this article attempted to prove, first, what many unhappy supporters of the North had often claimed – that the army was being run by incompetents. But the editor went beyond that and stated that these incompetents had been placed in their influential positions by deliberate intent. If a reader accepted this thesis, he must condemn Lincoln and Lincoln's generals as conspirators who would prevent the appointment of anyone with real ability to important military positions, and thereby unnecessarily prolong the war for political reasons. By extension then, *The New Nation's* readers who accepted this argument, must also accept the notion that Fremont was feared by the President as a potential rival, and as a result was being forced to languish inactive while the war effort stumbled on inconclusively.

Week after week Cluseret wrote articles, commentary and editorials in which he criticized all those who could possibly stand in Fremont's path to the presidency, either because they were direct opponents or rivals of Fremont or because they were too closely identified with Lincoln to be ignored. Pope, McClellen, Thomas, Sheridan, Sherman, and even Grant – none were spared.

Was Fremont was serious candidate? Lincoln's associates wrote him off as a mere stalking horse for Salmon P. Chase, also his public attitude of standoffishness tended to suggest that he was none too involved. In July, for instance, lest the public identify him too closely with *The New Nation* in which

---

57  Ibid. March 5, 12, 19, 1864

58  Ibid. March 19, 1864

pages Cluseret was clamorously waving his banner, he arranged for ownership of the paper to be lodged in the "National Pathfinders Association," a legal fiction, since Fremont defrayed most of its operating costs.[59]And, once when he was jointly interviewed by Wendell Phillips and Karl Peter Heinzen, one of his German supporters who was editor of the *Boston Pioneer*, he declared that he read *The New Nation* only after it was off the presses, as its editorial policy, he stated, was independent.

As the Republican candidate in 1856, Fremont had chosen not to participate actively in the campaign and in 1864 simply repeated the pattern. Neither he nor his followers however conceived of him as a mere front; his references to other candidates had the sole purpose of emphasizing his desire to see anyone but Lincoln as the standard bearer. Because of his habit of exclusion, his counsellors succeeded in convincing him to believe, at least up to the time of the Fremont nominating convention, and even to some extent after, that he had widespread popular support.[60]As for his attitude toward the paper, Cluseret complained that Fremont examined each week's editorial closely before approving, objected to the editor's habit of criticizing General Grant, forbade him to print a sharp critique of General McClellan's military performance, and once ordered a particular editorial excised at the last moment.[61]If Cluseret is to be believed, Fremont spent as much as $15,000 to $20,000 per month on the campaign.[62]

A strange action on the part of Fremont that Cluseret became aware of, was the Pathfinder, as an ardent abolitionist, courting the Democrats,[63]That he did so in some measure is not debatable, since his running mate was John B. Cochrane, the New York "War Democrat," How far he intended to go in this direction is open to doubt. Did he only want true "War Democrats?" or would he have taken up with any Democrat? Here Cluseret provides considerable

---

59    Cluseret to Sumner, Sept. 22, 1864

60    *The New Nation*, Sept. 24 and Oct. 8, 1864, Cluseret to Sumner, Sept. 22, 1864

61    Cluseret to Sumner, Sept. 22 and Dec 31, 1864; *The New Nation*, July 30, 1864

62    *The New Nation*, Sept. 24, 1864; *The New York Times*, quite well informed on developments within the Fremont campaign, reported on June 3, 1864, that Fremont paid the expenses of the delegates to his nominating convention.

63    Allan Nevins, *Fremont, Pathfinder of the West* (3rd. edition), New York, 1955) p. 571 and 574

enlightenment. As a precautionary measure against the eventuality of a falling out with Fremont, he saved two of the general's messages to him, copies of which he sent at a later date to the Senator from Massachusetts. These letters indicate that very early in the campaign, the explorer was hopeful of establishing ties with the Democrats, and that he was not adverse to support, if at all obtainable, from prominent members of the Democracy, who were not "War Democrats."[64]

During April, one of the periodic quarrels between the Republican press and the Democrats who ran New York City broke out. Chiefly involved were Parke Goodwin of the New York Evening Post and Horace Greeley of the New York Tribune against Judge George G. Bernard of the Tweed Ring.[65]On one occasion, the jurist in an *obiter dictum*[66] had offered sundry remarks concerning the war effort, which caused Godwin and Greeley to attack him editorially. This in turn led to a contempt charge against Greeley, which was quickly dropped.[67]Joining in, Cluseret had prepared an editorial for The *New Nation* lambasting the judge unmercifully, only to have Fremont veto it:

I have seen the article in *The New Nation* headed "Universal [sic] Scandal."

I beg you by no means to allow that article to be published. Judge Barnard is my friend politically as well as personally and the article would do great mischief.[68]

Fremont intervened on another occasion having to do with the attitude of the *New York World*, the cities' leading Democratic organ. The *World*, noting that the Fremonters were attacking Lincoln relentlessly, and realizing how advantageous this was to the Democrats, had taken to complimenting the Fremont candidacy.[69]Cluseret had intended to attack the *World*, feeling

---

64 Lowell L. Blaisdell, "Cluseret and the Fremont Campaign of 1864." *Mid-America*, Oct. 1964, Vol. 46, No. 4, p. 257

65 "William M. Tweed," in *Dictionary of American Biography*, ed. Dumas Malone, New York, 1936, XIX, p. 79-82

66 Remarks not on the point being considered

67 *New York Times*, April 8, 21, 26, 29, 1864

68 Fremont to Cluseret, n.d., enclosed in Cluseret to Sumner, Dec. 31, 1864

69 *New York World*, May 6, 30, 31 and June 2,7, 8, 11, 1864

that it "was doing us an immense damage by the species of hypocritical approval it gave," [70]only to have Fremont stop him: I think it will be best, looking at the course the *World* newspaper has taken that the article attacking it should not be published in *The New Nation*. The moment is critical and it might do mischief.[71]

However artful Cluseret may have been in his attempt to arouse some enthusiasm for Fremont however, the campaign never developed a significant following.

The great impetus to the Pathfinder's campaign was supposed to be provided by the vast popular gathering to be held in Cleveland on May 31 and June 1, in advance of the Republican convention. At the time, *The New Nation* applauded the "vast assemblage," the "unequalled unanimity," and the "great enthusiasm" that prevailed, whereas other newspapers described the conclave of about 400 as exceedingly unimpressive.[72]A "horrible fiasco," Cluseret called it subsequently. "Wrapped in self-imposed security," Fremont had been led to expect a great turnout:

General Fremont received up to the day even of the meeting, dispatches most adroitly combined, coming from the four points of the compass, announcing crowds of enthusiastic citizens. Two thousand men started from St. Louis and arrived but twenty-three in number. The *personal friend* of the General [Major Leonidas Haskell, with whom the editor engaged in a public quarrel] had attended to the transportation.[73]

The convention nominated Fremont and Cochrane, after drawing up a platform termed by the *New York Times* as "about equal parts of Abolition, Radicalism, and Copperhead cant."[74]"The Radical Democracy" as the new party was called, favored a one-tern presidency, strict enforcement of the Monroe Doctrine, Congressional Reconstruction, and, after confiscation of rebel land, its distribution among the voters. On the other hand, in deference

---

70   Cluseret to Sumner, Dec 31, 1864

71    Fremont to Cluseret, n.d., enclosed in Cluseret to Sumner, Dec. 31,1864

72   *New York Times*, June 2, 3, 1864

73   *The New Nation*, October 8, 1864

74   *New York Times*, June 3, 1864

to the Democrats' constitutional complains against Lincoln, there was a plank stating that free speech, *habeas corpus*, and a free press must be inviolate, and another settling the vital abolition question by announcing that since slavery had already been ended, only the enactment of a constitutional amendment was needed to formalize the fact.[75] In accepting the nomination, Fremont not only rejected confiscation of Confederate land plank, which further diluted the radical nature of the program, but also made an obvious play to the Democrats when, in referring to the convention's proposed constitutional amendment, he declared that "with this extinction of Slavery the party divisions created by it have disappeared."[76]

Had Fremont been in a position to secure the Democratic nomination, he might for a time have been able to scare Lincoln more than McClellan did by attracting some war-weary Republicans. In this connection, Cluseret recounted, "we have heard the editor of one of the most eminent organs of the Republican Party in New York say personally in our presence 'Let Chicago [the Democrats convention sight] nominate Fremont and we will all vote for Chicago.'"[77]

One of the major problems with Fremont connecting with the Democrats was the subject of abolitionism. There are some indications that Fremont would have liked his organ to veil or smudge over the glaring contrast between abolitionism and the Democracy. Unfortunately for him, with Cluseret, an extremist by temperament as editor, the dissimilarities were, if anything, only accentuated, since Cluseret took on the task of attacking the Lincoln administration with relish, because in his politics, he was an ardent abolitionist. Personally, he nursed a grudge against the incumbents as a result of alleged slights to his military skills while he was serving with the Union forces.[78] To the opposite task of carrying out Fremont's desire for feelers to the Democrats, he applied zeal if not conviction.

Week after week, Cluseret indicted Lincoln for a category of sins, real and

75   *The New Nation*, June 4, 1864

76   Edward McPherson, *The Political History of the United States of America during the Great Rebellion*, 2nd Ed., Washington, 1865, p. 410-416,

77   The New Nation, August 6, 1864. This was most probably a reference to Horace Greeley.

78   Ibid. July 2, 1864

imagined: lack of opposition to slavery throughout the land, Secretary of State Seward's failure to enforce the Monroe Doctrine in Mexico, the appointment of the incompetent General Grant as Commander-in-chief, reliance on pro slavery civilian aides and generals, the unequal treatment of Negroes, undue leniency to captured rebels, and systematic interference to with constitutional liberties, including freedom of the press.[79] Presumably the way to gain relief from so much wrongdoing was to vote for Fremont. Occasionally Cluseret even went so far as to hint at rebellion as the alternative, referring to the Fremonters as the "party of the oppressed" and urging: "On to the common enemy! Down with Lincoln.[80]

Warming to his topic, Cluseret showed considerable skill in the art of political writing between March and August of 1864 when he began to make observations about Lincoln's honesty:

Political catechism

What is a Copperhead?

A crawling animal

What is most like a copperhead?

Lincoln's administration.

Lincoln is the most unfit man in the nation for the Presidency.

As for Lincoln's policy, it is merely fatuity…to talk of that. No one talks of the absent or modifies what does not exist. To suffer one's self to be controlled by events was never a policy.

The *North American* is in favor of re-electing Mr. Lincoln for the very sensible reason that, though he is not particularly well qualified for the place, he might have done much worse; as a man might continue to employ a cook who continually spoiled his dinner, out of gratitude to her for not setting fire to his house.

---

79   *The New Nation*, March 19, April 2, April 16, April 23, May 21, June 11, June 18, 1864. These were standard Radical Republican charges of the time.

80   Ibid. June 18, 1864; the *New York Times*, July 4, 1864, specifically charged *The New Nation* with fomenting rebellion and giving aid and comfort to the Confederates

We are annoyed and irritated at hearing Abraham Lincoln and honesty always coupled together…to call one man "Honest" out of a population of thirty million, is not so much a complement to him as a sarcasm upon all the rest.

Mr. Lincoln's honesty is of a strange description. It consists of nearing ruining his country and in disregarding its interests in order to make sure of power for four years longer. To our eyes, the man who has deprived his country of the services of some of its best citizens, who has been unable to make use of incredible resources confided to him, and who, after agitating so many public questions without solving one of them, disregards his own utter incapacity is, of all the citizens of the United States, the least honest and the most dangerous.[81]

If Lincoln wasn't aware of *The New Nation* or of Cluseret, one of his supporters, a Frederick Driscoll who was a journalist and later a newspaper editor from Minnesota sent him a letter from New York City giving Lincoln information and his opinion about both:

(Private.)

New-York,

12th.April,'64

Sir,

I beg leave very respectfully, as a friend of your Administration, to give you some information about the organ of General Fremont and its conductors in this city, which may be of use to you.

A French fellow named Cluseret, and styling himself "General Cluseret", who was on Fremont's staff, is the head of the organ, which is named "The New Nation". This fellow can hardly speak a word of English and writes very bad French, yet he presumes to lecture us on our affairs! Being called into his office for a few days, in my capacity of French and Spanish translator, I have had the opportunity of seeing how "the organ" is conducted. Cluseret writes the military articles extolling Fremont (his master) and decrying every other

---

81  *The New Nation*, June 18, April 9, August 27, and March 12, 1864: the satiric observations on Lincoln's honesty are the best-known lines from Cluseret's newspaper; Carl Sandburg quoted part of them in *Abraham Lincoln*, 6 vols., New York, 1939, V, p. 71-72

general. He attempts politics occasionally, and then tries to draw a contrast between his chief and yourself very favorable to the former, and insulting to you. His writing is, per se, stuff; but it first passes through the hands of a translator, and then is refined (in composition, but not in subject) by a Mr. Briggs, who is virtual Editor of the paper, and is, I think, an emanation from the "World" office. The "organ" is got up for the election only, and cannot stand after that, (if Fremont be defeated), having no merit of its own. The funds to carry it on come from the pocket of Fremont, his tool, Cluseret, having no means of any account, being a mere French adventurer who does not care a straw for the good of this country, self-interest being his motives,--and who judged our affairs by those in France!

I am happy to say that the circulation of the "New Nation" is small.

If I can be of any service to you, you may command me.

I am, Sir,

Very Respectfully,
Frederick Driscoll.[82]

Cluseret while keeping up the harangue against Lincoln consistently flirted with the Democrats. One editorial, for instance, made an oblivious play for the votes of Irish immigrants in New York City by suggesting that they were being asked to fight for the Know Nothings, charging that the administration included "anti-Catholic" fanatics who desired to close the churches.[83]The Democrats were pictured rather favorably in contrast to the Republicans: "Aside to their adherence to slavery, which they are now somewhat reluctantly giving up, [the Democrats] certainly comprise the most intelligent and the most American portion of America." Or, "the Democratic party, defective as it is, is infinitely superior to the Republican party for it at least asserts person liberty and nation dignity." And, for example, "the Democrats must give up their attachment to slavery. The difference between the two parties is not as great as supposed.[84]Cluseret hammered away all through June, July, and

---

82    Abraham Lincoln Papers at the Library of Congress, Transcribed and Annotated by the Lincoln Studies Center, Knox College, Galesburg, Illinois.

83    Ibid. June 18, 1864

84    Ibid. April 23, June 11, August 20, 1864

August at the theme that the Democrats ought to nominate Fremont instead of McClellan; as the party had acquiesced in the nation's division, it could only hope to regain the voters' confidence by nominating a candidate well-known to stand for its union.[85] Carrying Fremont's tactic to its logical conclusion, the editor printed without comment a letter from a "Connecticut Democrat" urging Fremont's nomination at the forthcoming convention, but with the radical Democracy's anti-slavery plank dropped, thus offering an unbeatable candidate "untrammeled by instructions on slavery and the war."[86]

As the paper's letter columns started overflowing with criticism to the effect that if a small group of Radical Democrats were to combine with the greater part of the Democracy, the Radicals were certain to be mere captives, Cluseret countered rather unconvincingly that the superior virtue of the Fremonters' abolitionist program would be bound to capture the heart of all Democrats.[87]

During the summer of 1864, Cluseret did battle with both the *New York Tribune* and the *New York Times*. Henry Raymond, the *Times*' editor and Lincoln's campaign manager attributed Fremont's candidacy to "copperheadism or personal animosity," and the weeks passed, and as *The New Nation's* attacks continued, increasingly returned fire.[88] Never one to suffer attacks in silence, Cluseret resorted to choice invectives. The *Times* he labeled a "wretched organ of the administration"; to its complaint that Fremont was dishonorable in openly opposing Lincoln in wartime, "he rejoined: the editor of the *Times* talking of honor suggests the idea of a blind man criticizing a painting."[89] At the beginning of August, Cluseret struck at both of his newspaper adversaries:

The *Tribune* and the *Times* whose only remarkable feature is an equal degree of inconsistency hidden under a pompous display of wordy matter absolutely denuded of force, logic, or idea, distinguish themselves by a lavish profusion of epithets distributed left and right, and substituted in place of

---

85    Ibid. June 11, July 2, August 6,  20, 27, 1864

86    Ibid. June 18, 1864

87    Ibid. July 2, August 24, 1864

88    *New York Times*, June 7, July 4, 16, and 30, August 26, 1864

89    *The New Nation*, June 4, 11, 1864

reason and proof. Their epithets are like their bulletins of victory and their praises of Lincoln and Grant – they rest upon nothing, they are mere gas bubbles blown out into space, which vanish, leaving a pestiferous odor behind them.

For us, the first of the copperheads is Lincoln and his organ comes immediately after; we shall be careful in the future to restore them to the title which so justly belongs to them.[90]

By the end of August it became obvious that McClellan not Fremont would be the candidate of the Democracy. Simultaneously, some highly placed Republicans were seriously thinking of trying to sidetrack Lincoln and to hold a new convention at which another candidate would be chosen.[91]Fremont's reaction to this was an ambiguous half-turn back towards Republicanism. Asked to comment, he issued a written statement saying that he could not withdraw without the consent of his followers.

At the beginning of September, just after McClellan's nomination, a military event of great importance to the election campaign took place: General Sherman captured Atlanta. The stunning feat vastly increased the odds in favor of Lincoln's easy re-election. Nevertheless, the wheels of political intrigue that had been set in motion while the outcome on the battlefields was still dark kept on spinning for two or three weeks after that military turning point.

In the Fremont camp, Cluseret, although he supported his leader's pro-Democratic stance publicly, now that McClellan's nomination had been secured decided to make *The New Nation* "purely radical and independent."[92]This determination precipitated a split with his superior. Cluseret, after McClellan had been nominated, believed that Fremont, in order to end an "uncertainty that could only aid McClellan," ought to arrange his withdrawal as expeditiously as possible. He had had a conversation with Parke Goodwin, who was anti-Lincoln, and George Wilkes, editor of the pro-Fremont *Spirit of the Times*. Both had suggested that he ask the candidate-general if, in return

---

90   Ibid. August 6, 1864

91   Burton J. Hendrick, *Lincoln's War Cabinet*, Boston, 1946, p. 454-455

92   Cluseret to Sumner, Sept 1, 1864

for his stepping down, Fremont would "be satisfied with the replacement of [Montgomery] Blair by [Benjamin] Buttler [sic]" in Lincoln's official family. When Cluseret passed on this inquiry, Fremont answered "that he had a *better bargain*," and added, with reference to *The New Nation,* "say nothing against McClellan and pitch in [to] Lincoln." Cluseret responded that at Fremont's insistence, he had for six months refrained from directly attacking McClellan, but that he intended to do so at this time, in order to "fight McClellan and his abominable party blow by blow," and therefore he "could not comply with [Fremont's] desire."[93]This incident, which brought the candidate and his editor to a parting of the ways, occurred shortly after *The New Nation's* issue of September 10 had come off the press.[94]

As far as Fremont's remaining in the race was concerned, the strong peace platform drafted by the Democrats, coupled with a new turn in the North's military fortunes, was enough to cause those Radical Republicans who had not yet given their support to Lincoln to return to the fold and regard Fremont's candidacy as something too dangerous to ignore. With the cause of abolition hanging in the balance, nothing short of certainty would suffice. The Radicals therefore began to exert pressure on Fremont to withdraw. Zachariah Chandler, a strong anti-slavery senator from Michigan became an integral part of the conversations with both Lincoln and Fremont. As powerful as Chandler's pressure was however, Fremont did not announce his withdrawal immediately, more pressure was needed.

When it came, it emanated from within Fremont's camp and Cluseret supplied it, when it became clear to him that Lincoln, not Fremont would get the Republican nomination. The September 17 edition of *The New Nation* was an explosive one. Its main editorial, carried on the first page read as follows:

Some time ago we published in "The New Nation," that a day would come when General Fremont could suffer his interests to outweigh his principles, we should not hesitate to follow the principles and abandon the man. That day has come.

---

93   Ibid. Sept. 22, 1864. Italics in the original.

94   This can be deduced from the contents of the September 10th issue, which suggested that Butler replace Blair in the cabinet, and from the public news of the split reported in the *New York Times*, September 14, 1864, as having occurred on September 12

After having done all that was in our power to obtain from the Democratic Party the voluntary abandonment of slavery, the sole source, as well as the sole aim of the present war, begun and pursued by the South against the North – after the insolent reply of Chicago, not a shadow of a doubt, could remain in any loyal heart as to the course to follow. If we could not sustain Lincoln, we could not hesitate to oppose McClellan, the representative of the South, of foreign despotisms, and of slavery. Moved by the strong, unshaken, and immutable conviction of duty, urged by sincere affection and devotion, we represent to General Fremont that the moment had come to declare himself, and that, to hold the nation any longer in suspense, was neither wise nor patriotic; that he should either declare clearly his intention of running the risks of an independent canvass, which for the moment does not offer great chance of success, or abstain with regard to Lincoln, and combat McClellan. In any case to contend against McClellan was the first duty of every patriot and abolitionist. It was as such that Fremont was dear to us, and we thought that not a shadow of doubt could exist in his mind. We were deceived. General Fremont, entirely under the ascendancy of a man whom Democracy keeps near him to withdraw him from his principles and his friends, persisted in wishing to contend against Lincoln. Our conscience commands us to repudiate such bargains. We shall contend against McClellan, and, although the reelection of Mr. Lincoln may not be the best for the country, we do not hesitate to pronounce that the election of McClellan would be a great calamity...

Unfortunately, General Fremont listens to all the reports of any man who causes imaginary popular enthusiasm to glitter before his eyes, spends his money, profits by his natural indolence to cradle him in an illusion from which he will only awaken ruined in pocket and in reputation.[95]

On the day that this bombshell of Cluseret's exploded, Fremont wrote a letter announcing his withdrawal from the campaign.

In attempting to evaluate the impact of Cluseret's editorial, one must be aware of making too more of it. The effect of the pressure put on Fremont by the Radical Republicans must also be taken into account, even though there was a two-week gap between the meeting with Senator Chandler and

---

95    *The New Nation,* Sept. 17, 1864

Fremont. Similarly, if one supports the opinion that Fremont finally withdrew because he failed to make a deal with either Lincoln or the Democrats – and Cluseret gave credence to the notion that Fremont was indeed attempting to make such a deal – there are other questions. If all Fremont sought was Blair's removal why did he wait so long after it was promised before withdrawing? If he sought additional political favors why did he withdraw before he had secured them? The question of timing, which weakens the above theories, supports the conclusion that Cluseret's action may have been nothing more than the final blow but that in that capacity it was instrumental in securing what the Radicals wanted.

It is difficult to dismiss the fact that the September 17 edition of *The New Nation* appeared on the same day that Fremont wrote his letter of withdrawal as merely a matter of coincidence. It is doubly difficult to do so in view of the *Evening Post* revelation of an attempt by the National Pathfinder Association to oust Cluseret from his editorship on September 12 or 13.[96] Cluseret reported on the *Evening Post* story and claimed the ouster attempt was made because he had refused to support Fremont's candidacy any longer.[97] Thus Cluseret's editorial could not have taken the man he formerly championed unawares. Nor, because of the strong language Cluseret used and the somewhat surly tone Fremont adopted in his letter, it is possible to conceive that the two documents appeared simultaneously because of collusion between the two men.

To further substantiate the importance of Cluseret's act, there is testimony from the National Pathfinder Association. Unable to force Cluseret from his position and prevent the issuance of the September 17 edition of *The New Nation*, it was successful in eliminating him immediately afterwards. On October 8, there appeared an article in their journal entitled "American Generals and French Generals," a poorly done and heavy handed slap at Cluseret, which ended;

To be sure, we have among our officers no overshadowing military genius like Napoleon, unless it be Cluseret…The strategy in his campaign against Fremont was very remarkable. He hung on his flanks for a year or

96    *Evening Post*, Sept. 13, 1864

97    The New Nation, Sept. 17, 1864

so, devouring his substance and helping himself from his military chest, and the moment demonstrations were made against this exhaustive policy, with a French contempt of honor and truth, he killed him with a single coup.[98]

Thus the National Pathfinder Association was willing to place the entire blame on Cluseret. As a result, it seems apparent that whatever motives Fremont may have had that prompted him to leave the race, Cluseret's editorial was an important consideration, which, if nothing else, dictated the timing.

Fremont, rather than permit Cluseret to turn the weekly into a purely radical organ, went to court to obtain an injunction preventing continuance of the paper's publication by the Frenchman on the grounds that ownership and control were vested in the National Pathfinders Association, a company controlled by Fremont's associates, rather than Cluseret. The editor filed a counter-claim and got the injunction lifted, which allowed him to publish the paper.

During the fall, Cluseret published the paper on his own. In late September, he wrote Sumner that the New York City Democrats had offered him $30,000 for turning his paper into their organ.[99] This offer he somewhat reluctantly rejected, apparently believing that he had made such a spectacle of himself as an intransigent Radical that he could not, without suffering clamorous obloquy, turn a somersault. He hoped that the Republicans, in gratitude would see fit to compensate him to some extent, but having antagonized all of them by then, no reimbursement came forth.[100]Having nowhere else to go, he went on, unlike his erstwhile superior to campaign *for* Lincoln! Notwithstanding his announcement of the previous April that his candidate would "most certainly not be Abraham Lincoln, let him be whomsoever else he may," now he proclaimed, as election day drew near, "to have cast a vote for Abraham Lincoln in 1864 will be an act to boast of hereafter."[101]

---

98   Ibid. Oct. 8, 1864

99   Cluseret to Sumner, Sept. 28, 1864

100 *The New Nation*, September 28, 1864

101 *Ibid.* April 30 and October 29, 1864

With the election over, the paper folded. The Fremont experience closed a stage in the adventurer's life. He was forty-one years old, without work and without funds. The battle for *The New Nation* had cost him $1,148; worse his support of Fremont had cost him the trust of European friends and those who believed in him because they had always favored Lincoln's re-election.[102] Worst of all, Cluseret now believed that Fremont had turned his campaign into an attack on liberty throughout the world, by "prolonging an uncertainty which can only help [the cause of Democratic candidate] McClellan, which is to say, [the cause of] L [ouis] Napoleon, J [efferson] Davis, and black and white slavery."[103] Fortunately the American Republic retained a basic soundness: *Vox populi vox Dei*, he concluded when Lincoln won a second term.[104] He took stock of his position and concluded that he was now an American for good.[105] Because of this Cluseret began to sense disturbing parallels between America and France.

These parallels became clearer when he turned his attention to the problems of Reconstruction. By his own testimony, Cluseret had always been an abolitionist; in fact, he later boasted "in 1862, Jefferson Davis placed me outside the law...for having freed, on my own authority, the slaves at Madison Court House, [Virginia] without waiting for Lincoln's proclamation."[106] When the Emancipation Proclamation finally came he applauded it like "every cultivated man in Europe." Still it was not until 1864 that he began to correspond with Sumner about the fate of African Americans.[107]

In the early stages of the Fremont campaign, *The New Nation* followed a radical line on Reconstruction; calling for the confiscation of rebel lands, complete civil and political equality for the freedman, and constitutional guarantees of their rights. When Cluseret parted from Fremont, he kept these

---

102 Cluseret to Sumner, Sept. 22, Nov. 25, Dec. 31, 1864

103 Cluseret to Sumner, Sept. 22, 1864

104 "*The New Nation* to the Public," prospectus enclosed with Cluseret to Sumner, Nov. 10, 1864

105 Cluseret to Sumner, Nov. 15, 1864, Sept. 28, 1864, and Nov. 5, 1864, Sumner Papers, Vol. 139

106 Cluseret, *Memoires*, 2: p. 194, There is no proof that Jefferson Davis singled out Cluseret for condemnation, however, it is clear that he was in favor of abolition.

107 Cluseret to Sumner, Feb., 1864

political views. Nevertheless, he added his own. The Civil War, he told Sumner in late February 1864, was nothing but a result of the slaveholders' desire to perpetuate a "slave republic." By putting "slavery in the place of liberty," they had "attempted to invert the social pyramid from its natural base, attempting as in France to substitute authority for liberty!" Once they were defeated, the pyramid could be rebuilt on the solid foundation of freedman's liberties. But first the rebel leaders had to be punished, both as a matter of simply justice and an example to "Southern aristocrats." The slave-power could not be allowed to resurrect itself, or America might succumb to autocracy: this was a lesson that Cluseret drew from his own nation. Bourbonism was Bourbonism, he asserted, and "Lee's head like that of Louis XVI, must fall, judiciously, and in cold blood, in the name of law and morality.[108]

Leaving aside the rebel leaders, Cluseret went on to prescribe conditions for a durable emancipation of the slaves. Land was the most important consideration, and the easiest one to provide: simply confiscate it from the Southern masters and sell it off in small parcels to freedmen and Union veterans. This, he explained to Sumner, was "an analogy with our [French] revolution," whose history suggested "the best and least expensive army of occupation might be... [composed] of small proprietors implanted by a revolution into a newly conquered land."[109] The small proprietor, the yeoman, was also at the heart of the American revolutionary tradition, and Cluseret managed to evoke that tradition in the following passage:

The soil shall command the vote; therefore let us give the soil to our friends [the freedmen] and let the title of proprietor confer the title of elector without distinction of origin ... [I] the South [the cultivator] will be *ipso facto* a citizen and an elector.

"The vote for the blacks," he concluded, "is the revolution accomplished by the small proprietor and safe-guarded by him."[110]

The early months of 1865 were not an easy time for Cluseret, either personally or politically. Having developed his own plan for the "education,

---

108 Cluseret to Sumner, April 27, 1865

109 Cluseret to Sumner, April 16, 1865

110 Cluseret to Sumner, May 4, April 27, 1865

civilization, and definitive emancipation of the blacks through military organization," he watched the army instead become a tool of counterrevolution. Congress, he admonished the senator from Massachusetts, had ceded all policy initiative to "an executive [who would] weaken the revolution almost as much as if it had taken place in Paris." As a whole, the American political system had succumbed to corruption and vice. In short, "Yet another revolution miscarried."[111]

When Andrew Johnson became president, Cluseret became even less sanguine. Here we are," he wrote to Sumner on May 11, 1865, "in full counterrevolution. Virginia restored as a state by a president who considers himself the [sole] representative ... of the United States ...like Louis XIV saying *l'etat c'est moi.*" What was worse, Johnson's arbitrary policies had placed him on a par with Napoleon III, still the cynosure of evil in Cluseret's political universe. "Ah! Revolutionaries, you spit on your fathers and wish to be conservatives." The second American Revolution was lost.[112]

As far as what to do next was concerned, Cluseret had many schemes in mind, none of which materialized. One was to promote a national military school for training American general staff. Another was to lead a body of Negro troops against the South and then against Napoleon's forces in Mexico, under his leadership.[113] At one point, he thought of securing a position on one of the New York newspapers. He was almost frantic in his search for new employment.[114] He thought of requesting re-entry into the army, if he could claim American nationality according to a new law pending before Congress. Again and again he pleaded with Sumner to "make something of him."[115] But as yet, Sumner had no more than friendship to offer him.

In June 1865, Cluseret conceived the idea of issuing a new morning two-cent daily newspaper, which he saw as a way of becoming involved in the struggle over Reconstruction. By September of that year, he was well along

---

111 Cluseret to Sumner, November 10, 1864, February 3, February 23, March 1, 1865

112 Philip M. Katz, From Appomattox to Montmartre. Cambridge: *Harvard University Press,* 1998, p.10-13

113 Cluseret to Sumner, Nov. 15, 1864, Sumner Papers, Vol. 139

114 Cluseret to Sumner, Feb. 1, 1865, Sumner Papers, Vol. 140

115 Ibid.

with the project, but received little encouragement from Sumner.[116] For a year thereafter, Cluseret tried repeatedly but in vain to prod the Republican Party leadership into financing his newspaper project by reporting various efforts of the Democrats to buy his services.[117]

By the end of the summer of 1866, however, the note of demoralization, which had entered his letters to Sumner, had disappeared and was replaced by a tone of self-confidence. The change began at the end of April 1866, when a number of new projects were given to him by Sumner, taking him first to Mexico and then to Europe on secret missions connected with American expansionist ambitions and foreign policy.

Cluseret's connection with the Mexican question dated back to March 1865 when two of his friends, French officers returning from Mexico, provided him with confidential information on the status of Louis Napoleon's army in that country. He immediately conveyed the information to Sumner along with an unsigned article on Mexico that Cluseret wrote and published in *Army and Navy Journal* of July 29, 1865 which strongly suggested that the author had semi-official contacts. His correspondence with Sumner during this period indicated knowledge of the Government's intelligence projects relating to Mexico.[118]

This mission resulted in a book on the French invasion of Mexico entitled *Mexico and the Solidarity of Nations*. Directed against Louis Napoleon's adventure into the Western Hemisphere, the thesis of the book was based on the affirmation of the Monroe Doctrine, which, Cluseret said, involved the gravest question of the age and was destined to fix the battlefield upon which the principles of liberty and absolutism were bound to fight it out.[119]

To Cluseret, this meant not only American hegemony in the Western

---

116 He began thinking of this idea as early as September of 1864. See Cluseret to Sumner, Sept. 28, 1864, Sumner Papers, Vol. 139

117 Cluseret to Sumner, Dec. 20, 1865, Sumner Papers, Vol. 141

118 Cluseret to Sumner, Dec. 9, 1865, Sumner Papers, Vol. 140 in which he pleads with Sumner to send him to Mexico. See also "France and Mexico" unsigned article in the Army Navy Journal, July 29, 1865, pp. 4-5 ; 772-773; August 27, 1864-Aug. 19, 1865, New York Public Library. In his *Mexico and the Solidarity of Nations* (New York, 1866) p.12, Cluseret claims that he wrote this unsigned article.

119 Cluseret, *Mexico and the Solidarity of Nations*, p. 106

Hemisphere, but American domination of the world. In his opinion, it was America's destiny to republicanize the globe, and what he had in mind was not merely the extension of its ideological influence but, whenever possible, outright annexation. He did reveal this openly in his book, but he was forthright about it in his private correspondence with Sumner. In this respect, he was undoubtedly a jump ahead of Sumner; but he was in full harmony with the most aggressive expansionists among the new American bourgeoisie.

# The Fenians

The Mexican venture was barely out of the way when Cluseret embarked on a new task, this time connected with American-British rivalries. He became commander-in-chief of the Fenians for the uprising they planned to make in Ireland in 1867. His work on the Fenian project seems to have begun simultaneously with his Mexican assignment, since he placed an order for Henry rifles at the end of April 1866.[120]This may have been done for use in Mexico, but it was more likely done on behalf of the Fenians.

The Fenian movement as such was an Irish revolutionary people's movement, initiated by Irish revolutionary exiles in Paris in 1848. Its goal was the emancipation of Ireland from British rule and the establishment of an independent republic based on universal suffrage and peasant ownership of the land. It found strong support among the vast Irish immigrant population of the United States, where the American branch was first organized in 1863. The chief aim of the American arm of the group was to supply money and arms to the movement in Ireland.[121]

In the United States, however, the Federal Government was interested in the Fenian movement not only because of the Irish vote, but also allegedly because of its usefulness as a weapon in the struggle against England. As such, the Government had succeeded in capturing control of it and subordinating it largely to its own foreign policy purposes, as an example the Fenian raids into Canada in 1866 and again in 1877, even though the American army authorities disavowed the Fenian actions at the most crucial moment despite prior encouragement and support.[122]Cluseret's mission was directly related to

---

120  Cluseret to Sumner, undated letter, probably the beginning of April 1866

121  T.A. Jackson, *Ireland Her Own* (New York, 1947) p. 271

122  Major Henri Le Caron, *Twenty-Five Years in the Secret Service*. The Recollections of a Spy (London, 1892) p. 28, 31, 58-59. The British branded the Fenian movement as a "treasonable movement which was hatched in America." Lord C. Hamilton, House of

American interest in Fenianism.

As a public cover for his secret mission, Cluseret promptly secured a letter from Governor Reuben Fenton of New York assigning him to study the cost and utility of various militia systems in England and on the Continent. Before leaving for Europe, he also secured a letter of introduction from Sumner, together with a highly secret mission connected with American aims in the Eastern Mediterranean.[123] His task was to encourage pro-American movements and insurrections in the countries of the area

Louis Napoleon's spies, who followed Cluseret closely, promptly reported to Paris that in was in England "on a double mission confided to him by Mr. Seward" with the object of utilizing the Reform League, the Trades Union, and the Fenians "for the detriment of England."[124] Their information was sufficiently precise, despite numerous errors to suggest that they had a substantial basis for their report about Cluseret's official assignment.

Cluseret had met with James Stevens, the chief organizer for the Fenians or the Irish Republican Brotherhood (IRB) in New York City in May 1866. The IRB was a secret organization founded by Stevens and a handful of sympathizers in Dublin in March 1858. By 1865 it was the dominant force in Irish politics. This success was achieved in the face not only of British repression, but also of the bitter hostility of the urban middle class and large tenant farmers. During 1865 the IRB began to go into decline, weakened by arrests and victimizations, although it was still able to muster some thousands of supporters at the time of the abortive 1867 rising.

It is well known that the IRB despite being rooted in the Irish lower classes never adopted a social program. What is less well known is that among its leaders were men with an internationalist perspective on their struggle, including James Stevens himself. From the beginning, he was determined to ally the IRB with working-class radicalism in Britain, and went out of his way to recruit into its ranks Continental revolutionaries such as Gustave

---

Commons, June 26, 1867, reported in the London *Times,* June 27, 1867, p.6

123  Cluseret to Sumner, Nov.1, 1866. For Cluseret's secret assignment see his letters to Sumner beginning with March 27, 1867. That Cluseret's mission involved stirring up insurrections may be seen from his letter to Sumner, July 4, 1867

124  "General Cluseret's Dossier," *London Daily Telegraph,* April 24, 1871, p. 5

Cluseret.[125]After a meeting with Stevens, Cluseret reported:

"He [Stevens] was very clear and very explicit in his explanations. He was an organizer to the fingers' ends, and in this respect he was undoubtedly a man of superior merit; but he was vain, despotic, and overbearing beyond any man I ever saw. As regarded action, he was worth nothing. I left the house much disturbed in my mind. Stevens had explained to me, at great length and in much detail, the resources of the Fenian organization. He had given me a key to his organization, which did not leave out a single man in all Ireland; everything had been scrupulously and carefully visited and organized. As far as men were concerned, there no longer seemed need that any should be brought over. The whole of Ireland was enrolled in the organization, either actually or standing well affected towards it; and as this was his strong point, he was careful to furnish me with the most indubitable material proofs of the facts he stated.

"I was present at the meeting of various representatives of the most important Irish Centers. The report was made for the whole of Ireland, as is done for a regiment, each sergeant major reading the report of his company to the colonel. I was really astonished."

"But," remarked Cluseret, "men were not everything," money and arms were also requisite. Of money they had some; as to armament, the Frenchman confesses, what we have already pointed out, that they were miserably deficient therein. "They tried to dazzle me with representations of their further resources," adds Cluseret, which was a characteristic proceeding on the part of Stevens and his subordinates. Cluseret however was not to be deceived; he was determined to search the whole thing to the bottom, which he succeeded at last in reaching. Then he found "that the arms and ammunition existed only in imagination, or "-what was much the same-"in the arsenals"-of the enemy.[126]

Stephens and Cluseret calculated that England would not be able to concentrate more than thirty thousand men in Ireland. On this basis they

---

125 John Newsinger, "A great blow must be struck in Ireland: Karl Marx and the Fenians," *Race and Class*, 1982, 24:151, p. 156-157

126 John Rutherford, *The Secret History of The Fenian Conspiracy, its Origins, Objects, and Ramifications.* Vol. II, (London, C. Kegan Paul and Co., 1877) p. 256-257

believed that ten thousand men, resolute and acting on their own soil, "would be able to seize upon the most important points for embarkation and the principal roads of communication." These two sentences sum up the system of strategy that Cluseret resolved to adopt. In addition to seizing the strategically important points, he thought that these ten thousand men, moving rapidly, would draw after them the sympathizing multitude, and, with the aid of the latter, crush the English army in the field, before aid could arrive.

The figure of ten thousand became Cluseret's ultimatum. When that amount of manpower was raised, Cluseret would lead them, until then he refused to do more than draw up a plan of the campaign, based on the information that he had been given, and Stevens consented to the arrangement.

But if Cluseret would not take one step without his army of ten thousand, he was of another mind when it came to money. He insisted on receiving a large sum to begin with, and to be paid his salary from that day forward, when it was due. Stevens also complied with this stipulation, raising the money by selling the steamer Campo Bello, which had been returned to the Fenian Brotherhood by the government of the United States. Once the details were settled, Cluseret was appointed commander-in-chief of the Fenian army. He immediately hired two adventurers like himself, Octave Fariola, an Italian officer of engineers who became his Adjunct-General and Victor Vifquain, a Frenchman who was to be his Lieutenant-General, both had fought with him in the American Civil War.

Because of his search for allies, Stephens sent Cluseret to London to meet with the leaders of the Reform League, which had been fighting pitched battles with the British government since the summer of 1866, in their quest for an extension of the franchise to the working-class.

According to Howard Evans in his biography of William Randal Cremer, one of the Reform League leaders, Cluseret approached Cremer, Robert Hartwell, and George Odger and offered to put "at their disposal 2,000 Fenians armed and equipped with revolvers, with knives, and batons ferres, 500 of them also armed with carbines. According to Evans, the offer was declined because in the event of the British government conceding electoral reform, the insurrection would consist of only the Fenians and a few hundred workmen." However if reform was not forthcoming, then they "would gladly accept General Cluseret's offer." Cremer was later to deny that he offered Cluseret any encouragement.[127] Another leading figure in the Reform League, John Bedford Leno, provided a different account of Cluseret's approach.

> I received a circular from a well-known member of the Reform League calling upon me to attend a meeting at the White Horse, Rathbone Place, in order to meet M. Cluseret. On my arriving, I was shown into a private room, where I found a dozen of my conferees. The chairman announced the purport of our being called together. It was none other than to create civil war. Cluseret, who followed, said he was in a position to command at least two thousand sworn members of the Fenian body, and on our consenting to join him, would act as leader. I was the first person to attempt a reply, in which I denounced the proposal, stating that if we went ahead with it, it would surely lead to our discomfiture and transportation. I, moreover, stated it was my firm belief that the government would surely be made acquainted with our secret ...and declared my intention of getting out of the place as soon as possible. Others agreed with my view of the matter, and the room was soon cleared of those present.

According to Leno, George Odger was certainly one of those "favourable to the views of the French adventurer."[128]

Cluseret's own account described how he quickly became aware of the ill-preparedness of the movement in Ireland, where there was no shortage of men, but very few weapons. He pinned his hopes on an alliance with the Reform League: "I saw at once that I was on the wrong track, and that the Irish Question could only be settled by English co-operation." He went on:

> I met with sympathy as warm as Ireland and her federal enfranchisement amongst old Chartists to whom I had brought letters of introduction, as I did amongst members of the Reform League. I had even a nocturnal interview with members of the Executive Committee; in the course of which I was assured that if the Irish desired to join in hand with them, they would certainly be welcome; and that they would make a platform which would

---

127  Howard Evans, *Sir Randal Cremer* (London: Fisher Unwin, 1909) p. 46-47

128  John Bedford Leno, *The Aftermath* (London: Reeves and Turner, 1892) p. 71

be acceptable to both parties. I communicated these proposals to the most influential members of the Provisional Fenian Government. The most intelligent amongst them were of the opinion that it would be well to come to an understanding; others, the more narrow-minded, would listen to nothing except the "Irish Centers." I cut these short, and, taking with me men the most highly influential as well as belonging to the highest class in the Fenian hierarchy, I repaired with them to the house of one of the most important members of the Committee of the Reform League, and there the basis of an agreement between Fenianism and the Reform League was agreed upon.[129]

While there are oblivious discrepancies in these accounts, there can nevertheless be no doubt that the leaders of the Reform League did have substantive discussions with the Fenians and that some went further. It also seems clear that a number of leading British radicals were more prepared to consider the use of force to win the vote and to ally with the Fenians at this time then they would later care to admit. As far as Cluseret was concerned, it's credible that he believed some sort of violent confrontation between the British government and the Reform League to be inevitable. Any radical mass movement challenging a government on such a fundamental issue on the Continent was certain to be physically crushed; troops would be used to put it down and violent disorder would be the result. It was inconceivable that the government would actually give ground and even make concessions. In these circumstances a Reform League-Fenian alliance was almost bound to come about. He was of course confusing the realities of British politics with those of the Continent.[130]

Aside from the connection with The Reform League, there was along the possible link between the IRB and secret societies on the continent that worried the British government. James Stevens seemed to have derived his circle (or cell) system of organization for the IRB from his association with French secret societies: the Fenians had canvassed support from groups on the continent, and the British knew that they had hired foreign officers – Cluseret, Fariola, and Vifquain, to command the Fenian army during the rising.

---

129  Gustave Cluseret, "My Connection with Fenianism," *Littell's Living Age*, No. 114 (1872) p. 360

130  John Newsinger, *Fenianism in Mid-Victorian Britain* (London: Pluto Press, 1994) p. 53

While the British authorities doubted the commitment of these foreigners to the Fenian cause, the Chief Secretary for Ireland, the Earl of Mayo, argued that Fenian links to continental secret societies provided a compelling reason to continue the suspension of Habeas Corpus in Ireland. In his speech to the House of Commons, the Chief Secretary claimed:

[Cluseret and Fariola] were connected with the revolution on the Continent, and came to take advantage of the state of things in Ireland to create a rebellion, which if successful could only end in the uprooting of society, the destruction of property, and the overthrow of religion.

Mayo may have exaggerated the danger, but his speech illustrated the menace foreign revolutionaries added to Fenian unrest, particularly for an English audience accustomed to ridiculing Irish conspirators.[131]

Initially the rising in Ireland had been planned for February 11, 1867, it was postponed, but a breakaway faction went ahead with its own attack on Chester Castle in England to capture the arms stored there. The idea was to capture the munitions, then seize a ship and transport them to Ireland. When the plan had been betrayed, it was abandoned and rescheduled for March 5.

Because of the poor state of readiness of the Fenian military, Cluseret was convinced that a successful rising was not possible. While there were 15,000 sworn men ready to fight in Dublin, there were only 1,500 weapons with which to arm them, including pikes. Since the army available to the Fenian generals was reduced back to a mass of untrained regulars, to "men who are insubordinate by temperament, without organization, without any framework," believed Cluseret, who added, "This sort of thing wears our life quickly."[132]Despite this, Cluseret agreed to reduce to 5,000 the number of men that he required to be in the field before he would assume command:

I would not bind myself by any engagement, but I was inclined to make a beginning with five thousand men, thinking that some fortunate chance might furnish of striking some blow at the beginning, which might provide

---

131 Padraic C. Kennedy, "The Secret Service Department: A British Intelligence Bureau in Mid-Victorian London, September 1867 to April 1868," *Intelligence and National Security*, Vol. 18, No. 3 (Autumn, 2003) p. 108-109

132 Gustave Cluseret, *My Connection with Fenianism*, p. 361

us with resources; and, on the other hand, if the five thousand men could do nothing after being called together, there would evidently be nothing for it but to turn back, the victim of my own good intentions.[133]

He still hoped that something could be made of the situation, both in Ireland and in England with the Reform League. Because of that hope he produced a two-step plan of action. First would come a guerrilla operation, groups of armed patriots would fight the enemy in their own neighborhoods. These groups would be small in number, no more than fifteen or twenty men, the object being not only to take territory, but also to gain confidence in their military ability, even though the successes would be small. The groups were also to muster at strategic points in order to prevent the concentration of troops. Here they were to mass as strongly as possible, collect provisions, and throw up defenses. Meanwhile larger groups, numbering no more than five hundred were to scour the country, again staying in their own territory. The movements of these flying columns were to be based partly on the five or six detached mountain systems of Ireland, and partly on strategic points. They were to hold on to some of these points for defensive purposes and on others to receive supplies. In all quarters, their positions and areas were assigned so as to flank the main roads and thus to render the movement of the British columns difficult and dangerous. The plan showed that Cluseret understood his trade, and had studied the physical geography of the country. These detached mountain systems – in Antrim, Donegal, Connaught, Kerry, Cork, and Wicklow – with a great central depression, and lateral valleys branching out from the depression, as fingers branch out from the palm. A powerful invader seizing Dublin, the outlet of the central plain, and occupying that plain itself, could split up the country and overwhelm the nation's defenders if they attacked the invaders as an army. However, if the small groups in the field, cutting communications, attacking police barracks, and destroying local military detachments were successful, the second step would start, Cluseret would assume command and the transition to large-scale military operations would begin.

Cluseret's plan was the best possible under the circumstances; it allowed the rebels to act as guerrillas, only attempting to achieve the possible, and at the same time evading the superior British forces. The larger military actions

---

133  Ibid. p. 39

would not begin until there was success at the local level, and if the successes did not come the small groups could go underground, keeping the organization intact. In essence, Cluseret planned a "war of posts."[134] His only hope lay in prolonging the rebellion until some foreign power should intervene (the hope was that this power would be the United States). England, powerful as she was, and holding the central position, could keep the rebellion in check everywhere, while directing the mass of her army on the Irish centers, crushing them in succession. However, Cluseret's and Fariola's plans were ignored and the Irish provisional government in London appointed Godfrey Massey, an Irish-American, who had fought as a Colonel in the Civil War to command the Fenian forces in the initial phase of the rising. Instead of Cluseret's tactic of low-level guerrilla warfare, Massey, decided on an all out attack, which was supported by the Fenian leadership. This plan resulted in a debacle, the Fenian troops weakened state and poor level of armament could not support this type of warfare. Additionally, the rising was betrayed by a number of informers including Massey when he was told of the extent of British knowledge of the Irish plans. Fariola said of the new plan, "the Irish Republic was not to have any infancy and growth during which it would get beaks and talons. It was to be born full-grown and fully armed."

While the Fenian action in Ireland had collapsed, it was not the case in England. The organization remained intact and the alliance with the Reform League was still a possibility. On April 27, the *Commonwealth* newspaper warned the government that if they did not concede to working class demands, "there would be a war of the classes, a revolution" and the League might have the support of the Fenians.

Fenianism, so long as it is confined to Ireland might excite little or no alarm; but what would become of the ruling powers if the English democracy

---

134  While it is not known where Cluseret learned this particular method of warfare, it may have been from George Washington who used the same tactic after the Battle of Long Island "In deliberating on this Question [how best to fight the British], it was impossible to forget, that History, our own experience, the advice of our ablest Friends in Europe, the fears of the Enemy, and even the Declarations of Congress demonstrate, that on our Side the War should be defensive. It has even been called a War of Posts. That we should on all occasions avoid a general Action ...unless compelled by a necessity, into which we ought never to be drawn ...The honor of making a brave defense does not seem to be a sufficient stimulus, when the success is very doubtful." George Washington papers at the Library of Congress, 1741-1799: Series 3a, Varick Transcripts. Washington remained on the defensive and kept his army intact, the Irish ignored Cluseret and theirs was defeated.

were to shake hands with the democracy of Ireland …such a union has been more than hinted at.

The Reform League called for a demonstration on May 6 and as a result, 150,000 demonstrators filled Hyde Park and the government backed down, allowing the occupation of the park.

Cluseret was certain that if the government had chosen to suppress the demonstration by force, then "all the Fenians in London, who are many, would have withstood them like one man, and a good many resolute Englishmen would have aided them." In his opinion, the government "was well advised to let them alone…In France it would have been a revolution."[135]

When he realized that the projected uprising was impractical, he spent his time trying to convince some of the Fenian leaders of its futility:

> The dominant motive for the rising was more probably a feeling among the Fenians, both high and low, that the movement could not depart gracefully without some unequivocal gesture to honor its bold promises and to fix its defeated principles unmistakably in the record of history. Like Emmet and Rossa in Green Street Courthouse, they thought it unmanly to go down without a scene. Stevens had talked forevermore about the difference between the "spouters" and the doers, but the difference had never been acted out. Until it was, the Fenians were denounced by their own words as spouters of an especially contemptible breed. If Stevens was not sensitive to that logic, his successors were. Such at least was their reply to Cluseret when he pleaded with them to abandon an enterprise in which there was not one chance in a hundred, or in twenty hundred, of success. "My dear General," he reported them saying, "we are not under the smallest illusion as to what awaits us; but the word of an Irishman, once given, is sacred. Stephens has pledged us to this undertaking without consulting us, but we will keep our word, even though he may not keep his; and the people will know that, if there are some men who deceive them, there are others who know how to die for them."[136]

---

135   Ibid, p. 56-57

136   Gustave-Paul Cluseret, "My Connection with Fenianism," p. 205

Dissention to the leadership and betrayal resulted in the collapse of the rising however and Cluseret fled to Paris in order to escape arrest by the British.[137]

Why did Cluseret become involved in the Irish situation to begin with? Was it because he needed the money? After all, he had spent all that he had in the campaign with Fremont, and had pressed Stevens hard for money to join the Fenians, or was it the reasons that he put forth in *My Connection with Fenianism:*

As regards myself, I did not show more wisdom or foresight than the rest. As soon as I heard the discharge of the first gun, being completely ignorant of the real condition of things, I offered my services to the Fenians. Their "Head Centre" and co-President of the Great Council who kept a store for the sale of *nouveautes* in Bowery Street, New York, called himself Colonel X. Everybody was a colonel in those days, so the designation will not compromise anyone.

I was induced to take this course from two motives. The first, if the truth must be told, was the same that impelled the Irish to cross the frontier – the love of gunpowder. I had not that delight for two years. The second motive was more serious. In the Irish cause it was not Ireland alone that I saw, but humanity itself. I do not think of my fellow-creatures as so many Austrians, Germans, Poles, Russians, or any other nationality. They are all men, who, although by the chances of birth they have been born in different localities, have all alike the duties and the rights of a common humanity, and whoever infringes upon the rights of one man infringes on the rights of all.[138]

He believed that he was sent to deliver a "dose of Fenianism" to England,[139]but finding the means entirely inadequate, he had no intention of completing an impossible job. His complaint to Sumner about the affair a few weeks later left little doubt that his "indignation" was directed, not so much at the "truckling schemers" within the Fenian camp as at the United States government which he felt let the project down.[140]

---

137  Ibid. p. 37-42

138  Ibid. p 32

139  Cluseret to Sumner, May 24, 1867

140  Cluseret to Sumner, March 27, 1867

In the same letter to Sumner, Cluseret stated that the rising could have been successful:

> I know, (and) you know it, the whole Irish movement better than those who are nominally at the head of it. I can affirm to you that if we had had, on March 7, $100,000 in the treasury, the movement would have succeeded. It failed momentarily because of the total lack of money at the point where certain bands known to me had to receive the order to disband because of lack of money to pay the chiefs who were supposed to take command, Is an intelligent government in America not interested in destroying English aristocracy?[141]

Cluseret's return to French soil had not altered his conception of himself as an American[142]He expected to be back in the United States in the early part of 1868. In the meantime he began to work on his confidential mission, launched a magazine called *Art*, and busied himself with writing Sumner's biography.[143]When Cluseret attacked the military budget of the French government and predicted that war between France and Prussia was inevitable in the magazine *Le Courrier Francais*, the government retaliated by confiscating the existing issues of his magazine, and additionally, the pro-government organs bitterly denounced him. It was at this time that he wrote to Sumner: "We [Americans] are the only strong ones at the moment. If we move, the earth trembles. Ten months after we have affixed our seal to the bottom of a letter of marque, not a single government would be standing in Europe." The Europeans, he added, would run the governments and their own commerce under the American flag. Moreover, they could not do a thing against the Americans. As soon as their commerce stopped, their shops would close up and this would cause them to do "our job of insurrection." Immigration would then come to the United States *en masse*. All this, Cluseret insisted, belonged to the United States by right of civilization.[144]"It must advance and accomplish its mission of redeeming humanity. It must endow

---

141  Ibid.

142  He had become an American citizen during his Civil War service.

143  Cluseret to Sumner, May 24, 1867

144  Cluseret to Sumner, July 4, 1867

the world with its superior institutions.[145]

In Cluseret's opinion, the "old worm eaten European edifice" was "cracking up everywhere,"[146]and with war between France and Prussia a certainty, he was convinced that the opportunity was now at hand for the United States to exert its power. He was anxious, therefore that it overcome its internal complications over Reconstruction so that it could take full advantage of the situation; and he urged Sumner to press for action.[147]

Earlier in the year, Cluseret had run afoul of the French government for criticizing its military budget, now in September, he took up the issue of the reorganization of the French army and found it lacking. Borrowing many of his arguments from Sumner and informing him that his critiques would "include all the subjects that interest *us*." If the government persecutes me," he told Sumner, "I will fall back on my status as an American and will not leave the argument …I erected the flag of our party and of our country here. I will preserve it here against the whole world.[148]

The persecution that he may have been expecting came in February of 1868, when the French government finally hauled Cluseret into court and challenged his right to call himself a general, and he was on his own – despite his expectations of American backing, there was no word of encouragement from Sumner. Nor did the United States seem willing to grasp the opportunity Cluseret saw beckoning. The French judge made him produce his service documents justifying his title. "I could have stopped him short," Cluseret reported to Sumner, "by declaring to him that I was an American and by sending him to Dix [the American minister to France, General John A. Dix]. But on the one hand Dix is an old fogey, and on the other hand, I do not wish to unmask myself yet.[149]

Cluseret was also involved in two other situations at this time. He wrote to Sumner that he was acquiring "a great popularity" and the people wanted

---

145   Cluseret to Sumner, July 7, 1867

146   Cluseret to Sumner, July 7, 1867

147   Cluseret to Sumner, Aug. 19, 1867

148   Cluseret to Sumner, Sept. 6, 1867

149   Cluseret to Sumner, Feb. 14, 1868

to elect him to the Chamber of Deputies. "What is serious," he confided to Sumner, "is, in one respect, the well-known character of my opinions and especially my Americanism. Since the elections will not take place before a certain time and meanwhile I will have seen you, we shall talk."[150]He was also on a mission for Sumner in connection with Serbia and Montenegro.

I am expecting the envoys of the former country; I believe I am in accord with the latter. If my combination succeeds, we shall be a part without striking a blow and with out dipping into our pocketbook. I am confiding to you on your honor because I haven't even spoken about it to my ... [illegible] in order not to involve anyone. Things that are aired never succeed. There is a situation to take there and it must not be allowed to escape.[151]

In a subsequent letter to Sumner, he elaborated somewhat on the American "part" for which he and others were secretly working. "The truth is," he wrote, "that we want to establish at Constantinople a Danubian Federation like ours in which Montendgro, Serbia, Herzogovina, Bulgaria, etc., will participate in the same way as Massachusetts, N.Y., Pa., R.I. do[152]

Before this report to Sumner however Cluseret was deeply involved in his confidential mission and while there had been no further progress during the spring of 1868, he deferred his return to the United States because he believed that the situation could change quickly. His next letter to Sumner bore this out:

"You would not believe, I repeat, the influence of our country that is growing daily here. They people feel that they are in our hands. The peoples hope and the governments tremble. Farragut is their nightmare. Cost what it may, we must have a port in the Mediterranean and we shall have it in '69 through the Eastern question that is more and more attracting my attention. I shall tell you about this in detail next month in Boston because I expect to leave in June with Darling and his family

---

150   Cluseret to Sumner, Feb. 14, 1868

151   Cluseret to Sumner, March 12, 1868

152   Cluseret to Sumner, Jan. 13, 1869. If the phrase "like ours" refers to the United States, which it seems to, Cluseret has mixed up the American democratic republic with the Danubian Federation which is usually defined as a democratic super-monarchy.

whom I am expecting any day from Constantinople." [153]

However, Cluseret couldn't leave France. In July 1868, Louis Napoleon's government arrested him and sentenced him to two months in prison for the articles he had written in his magazine. To avoid the sentence, Cluseret appealed to anyone who he believed could help him. First, he tried Ambassador Dix, but Dix was occupied "only with himself and his railroad," and would not, "perform his duty toward an American citizen." Next was an appeal to "the people of New York," and to its governor, Reuben Fenton, and finally to Representative Ben Butler of Massachusetts and to Sumner.[154]"Let us try to understand for once our power and our destiny," he wrote to Sumner, "We alone in this world are strong. We along ignore our power. Our diplomatic agents more than anybody else, it should be time, however, to have agents abroad worthy of the name."[155]

As if to emphasize the value that he would be to the United States if he was not in jail, Cluseret reminded Sumner a week later: "War will break out any moment. Ah! If we don't profit from it, step into the midst of it, we will be precious simpletons."[156]Cluseret trusted in Sumner's promise to him in 1864 that as soon as the Civil War was over, the United States would pay its debt to the monarchies of Europe. Four years later, the promise was forgotten, Cluseret had to serve his sentence.

By the beginning of 1869, Cluseret was extremely pessimistic about the likelihood that the United States would take advantage of the situation in Europe. "We are about to lose everything that our victories had given us in public opinion," he warned Sumner on January 13, 1869. "You will never make the European people understand the egoism of Washington. Everyone for himself, everyone to himself. This policy, intelligent at the birth of the nation, is inept today when the American republic is alone able to dictate its will." Europe, he said, was ripe for revolution and waiting for the United States to move. "And parenthetically, we ought to finish with Cuba and generally all the Antilles to which we are entitled geographically and morally

---

153 Cluseret to Sumner, undated letter, probably between March and April, 1868

154 Cluseret to Sumner, end of July, 1868

155 Ibid.

156 Cluseret to Sumner, Aug. 7, 1868

by right of civilization." There was no danger from Britain, he continued, because the Fenians and the British republicans would promptly compel it to withdraw its forces. Russia and Prussia were the only powers relatively strong. The United States was on good terms with both of them, and he did not advise that these powers be provoked at the moment. But, he asked, what interest did it have in catering to Napoleon III, "this mortal enemy of liberty and human dignity, this man who has sustained Jeff Davis and after him Johnson, this man whose money was at 12 Wall Street, at Tilden's and $2000 of which I had refused in '64?"[157]

"The only diplomacy for the United States was force," Cluseret said, and, ridiculing Seward's weakness, he exclaimed: "Fortunately Grant is rougher …I urge you strongly to throw the full weight of you influence in favor of Greece and to distain the clamoring of Russia …the fruit [in the Balkans] is ripe and we are going to pick it. Moreover, that will be the best road against Russia."[158]

In March of 1869, Cluseret was trying to gain an appointment from Sumner as American diplomatic representative to Athens or Belgrade:

More than ever [he wrote] we need diplomats in Europe who are, above all, men of action and are well-informed about Europe. I mean by this men who know fundamentally all the threads of European politics, its tricks and its weaknesses. If we had in the East a man who was well informed on the East, France, and England, we would be the masters in the East and in all Europe because the masses and public opinion are for us. Now next year, the Isthmus of Suez will be an accomplished fact and our flag should float in the Mediterranean…[159]

He was particularly anxious that the United States should not forfeit its opportunity in Greece. He told Sumner that "the independence of Greece under our protectorate would be the most magnificent triumph we could dream of for our European policy. It is an occasion which perhaps will not present itself ever again." But Cluseret was not sure that Americans

---

157 Cluseret to Sumner, Jan. 13, 1869

158 Ibid.

159 Cluseret to Sumner, March 7, 1869

would understand this. "Thanks to our poor diplomacy," he lamented, "this magnificent Eastern complication from which we should have emerged as the first people of the world, master of European destiny, without firing a shot, will all finish up to the satisfaction of Napoleon III."[160]

Toward the end of May 1869, Cluseret came into conflict with the French government on a new issue involving some of its ministers. It was in connection with Fremont's old scheme to swindle French investors through the sale of his Transcontinental Railroad Bonds for which the Pathfinder was finally to be tried and convicted in 1873.[161] Seeing an opportunity to avenge himself for his costly partnership with Fremont in 1864, Cluseret seized upon the scandal and promptly attacked his former associate. As a result, an Imperial degree was issued by the French government ordering his expulsion from the country on the grounds that of obnoxious activity and the fact that he was no longer a French citizen.[162]

Cluseret appealed the order, and an agreement was signed by Elihu Washburne, the new ambassador to France with the French foreign office, according to which Cluseret agreed to leave the country in eight days. On the appointed day, Cluseret requested and with Washburn's help secured a two-week extension. A week before Cluseret's departure, Washburn sent a letter to President Grant through the Secretary of State Hamilton Fish from Cluseret protesting the actions of the French government in expelling him.[163] All of this was to no avail and on June 10, 1869, Cluseret left for America.[164]

This insult to his dignity rankled Cluseret; and the moment that he arrived, he renewed his protests to the State department. He intended to see Grant; but first he sent Sumner a note announcing his arrival and requesting to see him before calling on the president. Sumner was slow to reply to

---

160 Cluseret to Sumner, undated letter, written before June, 1869

161 Cluseret to Sumner, April 4, 1863 ("Poor Fremont who robbed me in 1864" was sentenced by the French to three years in prison for fraud.)

162 Cluseret, Memoires, III, P35-38

163 Cluseret to Hamilton Fish, Aug. 7, 1869

164 Once again Cluseret was not supported by the powers in Washington. Fish replied to Cluseret on August 10, 1869, acknowledging receipt of his letter on the subject of his expulsion and further stating that Washburn had not regarded Cluseret's complaints of sufficient importance to justify protesting to the French government.

Cluseret and finally contacted him in late August. Cluseret then replied and arranged to spend an entire day with Sumner in Boston to review Cluseret's work.

One of the chief topics of conversation was the administration's plan to annex Cuba. On this issue, Sumner did not agree with the president and Cluseret did. By temperament and outlook, the Frenchman was closer to a military man like Grant whose blunt buccaneering aggressiveness was so well suited to the new expansionist perspective, than to a cautious intellectual politician like Sumner. Sumner objected to recognition of the Cuban revolutionaries or any interference in Cuba, chiefly because of the reports of American agents on the island who believed that the situation was unfavorable to the United States because any action by the country would lead to British intervention which would be a menace to American shipping interests. Cluseret was impatient and indignant at Sumner's obstruction of American dominance of Cuba. On September 7, he wrote to Sumner, "I return to our conversation relative to Cuba ...I prefer the protectorate to annexation."[165]

Recognition of the Cuban revolutionaries, Cluseret insisted would not invite intervention by the British and would not be inconsistent. Furthermore, how could a second-rate power, "cause the foremost power of the world to retreat in fulfillment of its destiny by menacing the interests of a few rich ship owners, interests, mind you, which I do not at all believe to be menaced?"[166]

Then too, Cluseret continued, the reports of the American agents in Cuba were clearly unreliable; Cluseret then proposed to go to Cuba himself, at his own risk, to review the situation. It was Cluseret told Sumner in his political interest to send him to Cuba and to use the trip as the basis for a bold new policy. Nevertheless, Cluseret knew that Sumner would not be moved and warned him that he would regret his position bitterly.[167]

The Cuban insurrection, however, was only one of Cluseret's concerns during the year he was to remain in the United States. As usual, he had many

---

165  Cluseret to Sumner, Sept. 7, 1869

166  Ibid.

167  Cluseret to Sumner, Sept. 13, 1869

irons in the fire. He followed up on the fight against Fremont, but spent most of his time involved with the International Workingman's Association in New York. This was a new interest whose importance for his future ambitions had seem increasingly apparent to him since his Fenian adventure, but especially after 1868 when he met Eugene Varlin[168] and other leaders of the International[169] in Sainte Pelagie prison

When the Franco-Prussian war broke out after the Emperor of France declared war on Prussia, Cluseret immediately returned to Europe, arriving at Ostend, Belgium on August 18, 1870.[170]From there, despite his professed hostility to the French Empire, he telegraphed General Palikao,[171] placing himself at the disposal of "the organizers or the national defense." But there was no reply to his offer.[172]

Following the Revolution of September 4, 1870,[173]Cluseret reentered France. Here he again attempted to rejoin the French military by approaching General Louis Jules Trochu, the military governor of Paris and President of the Government of National Defense, who also refused Cluseret's services. Turned down twice for a military position, Cluseret went back to journalism. He had been in Paris for only a short time when his writings produced an uproar. Writing in the revolutionary *Marseillaise*, Cluseret attacked Leon Gambetta, a well-known French legislator for not arming the popular battalions of the National Guard. In his article *La Reaction* he accused Gambetta of effectively helping the Prussians by mistrusting the French proletariat, a most serious charge. Although during the Commune of 1871 such remarks would have been regarded as a truism, in September 1870, Cluseret was ahead of his time and his writing too radical in tone. A crowd of people from the town of Belleville – later the cradle of the Commune – burst into the offices of the

---

168  A French Socialist, Communard, and a pioneer of French syndicalism.

169  An organization which aimed at uniting a variety of different left-wing socialist, communist, and anarchist political groups and trade unions that were based on class struggle.

170  Cluseret, *Memories*, III, 6

171  Charles Guillaume Marie Appolinaire Cousin Montauban, comte de Palikao. The president of the council or Prime Minister who was reorganizing the French army.

172  Cluseret, Memories, III, 6

173  This bloodless revolution toppled the Second Empire and instituted the Third Republic

Marseillaise and burned copies of the offending issue. Cluseret was forced to backtrack and pacified the crowd by claiming that his attack on Gambetta was purely personal, which seemed to satisfy them.

Cluseret then attempted to create a solid position for himself by touring the political clubs of Belleville, Montmartre, and Les Halles. However, he was unsuccessful because another writer Henri Rochefort, the most successful journalistic opponent of the Second Empire accused him in the *Journal Officiel* of having incited the people to civil war.

Finding that his military skills were not in demand and his journalistic ones suspect at the capital, Cluseret departed for the Southern city of Lyons. Like Paris, Lyons had its own full share of socialists, neo-Jacobins, and local patriots. Like their Parisian counterparts, they saw the collapse of the imperial regime as a perfect opportunity to create a revolutionary Commune (i.e. a self-governing municipality, organized on democratic principles, and rather loosely affiliated with the rest of the nation as part of a federal polity). One of the advisors in this project was the Russian anarchist Mikhail Bakunin. He and the other would-be Communards in Lyons knew Cluseret by reputation, and they invited the general to lead their troops when the revolution came, which he quickly agreed to do. But when the fateful day arrived, September 28, 1870, it turned out to be a fiasco.[174]

Before Cluseret could begin to create a military force in the city, a crowd of workers stormed the Hotel de Ville (City Hall) and peacefully disarmed the troops on guard. Unfortunately, the workers were acting without any leaders, and no one on the scene knew what to do next. Their first thought was to ask Cluseret to guide them, but being a stranger to Lyons, he refused. As he later explained.

It was evident [even then] that this was only a fetus and not a new born, an impulsive act or, perhaps worse, [the act] of some agitator, the only possible result being …a mess. Seeing that nothing had been decided, neither a program nor its personnel, the best thing was to leave well enough alone.

---

174   According to Cluseret, he was "sent to Lyons by the [Parisian] Committee of the Twenty Arrondissements," a revolutionary group that later played a key role in initiating the Paris Commune. Cluseret, *Memories*, II, p.137

Which is what I did.[175]

All in all, it turned out to be a wise decision, for within twenty-four hours the local authorities had suppressed any further hint of an uprising, however these same authorities under the control of Leon Gambetta, Cluseret's nemeses from Paris drove him out of Lyons to Switzerland, where he took refuge.

The next individual that Cluseret comes in contact with was perhaps the oddest of all; this was George Francis Train an American who went from being an innovative capitalist to an outspoken radical to a certified lunatic. In the 1840s and 1850s, Train made several fortunes in gold, trans-Pacific shipping, British street cars, and the financing of the transcontinental railroad. The American Civil War took him to England where he agitated on behalf of the Union cause. Back in the United States, he supported the views of vegetarians and the feminists. He backed Elizabeth Cady Stanton and Susan B. Anthony financially when they began to publish their *Revolution* in 1868. He even joined them on the stump to campaign for women's rights. In 1872, he combined forces with Victoria Woodhull, the free love advocate, to battle Anthony Comstock and his bluenose crusade; resulting in a prison sentence, not the first one that Train had suffered. In later years a New York court would find him *non compos mentis*, and he would spend the rest of his life railing against the system and chatting with toddlers, birds, and squirrels.[176]

At this time (1870) Train was in the midst of a trip around the world that would later become the model for Jules Verne's famous tale. On October 20, Train's ship docked at the port of Marseilles, where he was pleasantly surprised to find a large crowd awaiting his arrival. They apparently knew about his support not only for the Fenians, but also for popular uprisings in Italy and Australia, and they greeted him as a liberator. Train was more than willing to accept the title and the responsibility that came with it, as he explained to a large crowd of workers that night. Introducing himself as "a citizen of the American Republic," he reminded them of the powerful ties that had always existed between the United States and France, from Lafayette to the present. He offered the crowd guns and "the moral force ... [of] a great

175 *Memories*, II, p. 138-139

176 Willis Thornton, *The Nine Lives of Citizen Train*, (New York, 1948)

people" to fight against the Prussians and to march on Paris. "The Republic in itself is an army," he told them, "and all Europe fears it ... if one must fight and die, let it be for liberty and France."[177]

Train wrote that he was immediately "possessed by the French revolutionary spirit. The fire and enthusiasm swept me from my feet. I was henceforth a Communist, a member of their Red Republic." Unfortunately for the crowd of rebels, he couldn't give them the promised guns. What he did give them was his advice, his belief in their cause, and his aid in getting Cluseret to come back from Switzerland to lead their *Ligue du Midi*.[178]Train knew of Cluseret because of their mutual interest in the International and the Fenian movement. Train therefore became part of a committee charged with sending a message to Cluseret in Geneva, asking him to take command of the local units of the National Guard in the name of the Ligue du Midi. Cluseret agreed, stipulating that he would need a certain number of armed men, not the 10,000 that he initially wanted in Ireland, but 2,000 here in Marseilles.[179]The committee agreed and Cluseret joined the National Guard in Marseilles. The result however matched that of Lyons. No sooner had the uprising begun then it was stopped three days later (November 3, 1870) by the central government. Cluseret escaped from Marseilles, chased through Southern France, by the French police keeping in touch with the International in Paris through Eugene Varlin.

---

177  George Francis Train, *My Life in Many States and in Foreign Lands* (New York: D. Appleton and Company, 1902) p. 302-305.

178  The League of the South, a republican committee formed in Marseilles in 1870 with the aim of defending the Third Republic. The *Ligue* was also an affiliate of the First International.

179  Train, p. 303-309

# The Paris Commune

Cluseret was not in Paris during the first clash between the Parisian revolutionary forces and the central government. When he arrived in a few days later, the city was already under the control of the National Guard,[180] and the provisional French government had fled to Versailles, both sides preparing for civil war. The Central Committee (part of the National Guard including patriotic Republicans and the Socialists) was in charge of the defense of Paris and as Cluseret assessed the situation, he saw that the Central Committee had committed four blunders: First, to allow the army of Paris to leave. He believed that these troops, even though they were initially against the Commune would eventually join the revolution if they were allowed to mix with the citizens of Paris. The second fault was in not occupying Mont Valerien. This fortress defended Paris during the Franco-Prussian War and was the strongest fortress defending the city. The third fault was in not immediately occupying the National Bank, which in the heart of Paris, carried on its operations against the Commune and paid its enemies. The fourth blunder was in permitting a resistance to the Commune to be organized in Paris.

Cluseret was asked to take command of the National Guards on the say he arrived in Paris, but refused for the following reasons, "I had no clear insight into the situation. Everything was new to me. I knew nothing about the National Guards or their resources; what little I had seen had given me much cause for reflection. Out of all the canon ranged in front of the Hotel de Ville[181]- and there were more than a hundred there – only four were fit for use. The ammunition, such as it was, was totally insufficient; the projectiles were not of the right caliber; the breeches did not act."[182]

---

180   The Citizens Militia

181   City Hall

182   Gustave Cluseret, "The Military Side of the Commune." *The Fortnightly Review,* No. LXXIX, New Series,- July 1, 1873, p. 3

As far as the Central Committee's military force was concerned, the artillery gunners were good marksmen, but useless, because as volunteers, they were not subject to orders and as a result came and went as they pleased. The cavalry horses Cluseret termed scarecrows and therefore were scarcely fit for escort duty. The greatest military problem was the infantry, who he believed, to be good fighters, but leaderless. Their officers were competent in a political sense, but not in a military one, and this was the upcoming phase of the revolution. Their generals were decorated with lace and stars, and were in fact worth less than the soldiers whom they commanded. To Cluseret, they had substituted morale for competence – "They believed in enthusiasm, in masses, in crowds of people of both sexes marching on Versailles, some on horseback, some riding on canons, and singing the Marseillaise."[183]

During the period of time between March 22, 1871 and April 2, 1871, Cluseret's position was one of military advisor to the Central Committee, but on that day in April, the war between the Communists and the French government at Versailles commenced with the shelling of the city from Mont Valerien. While this opening action was only a skirmish, it revealed, on the one hand the intention of Versailes, and on the other the condition of the poorly led National Guards, who, taken by surprise, fled in disorder. That afternoon, Cluseret was given the post of Minister of War. Immediately, he received two pieces of bad news; one, that the forces that he had just been given were on the attack, and secondly, that he could do nothing about it. The Communard's military was commanded by three improvised generals, only one of whom had any military experience and that was as a sergeant. The next morning Cluseret set out to prevent the coming disaster. Even though the Communard army consisted of only 60,000 men as opposed to the 200,000 that they had on paper, they were able to initially hold their own, due to the incompetence of the Versailles forces and the arrival of Cluseret. However by April 4, the National Guard ceased to be an organized body, destroyed to the point that there was no ability left to take the offensive. Cluseret compared it to the rout at Bull Run in 1862. The Commune also wanted to create the post of Delegate for Exterior Relations, which was opposed by Cluseret, "Of what use was a delegate for foreign affairs to a municipal? It was above all necessary to avoid anything that could have given a false impression in

---

183 Ibid. p. 4

this matter."[184] This was important to Cluseret because in his negotiations with German officials he insisted: "We are by no means making a national revolution; it is a municipal movement, nothing more."[185] Nevertheless, the situation left Cluseret with two tasks – reorganization and concentration: the abandonment of positions which could no longer be defended and the concentration of the Commune on their remaining positions, because the Commune's military role was no longer one of conquest. First, he ordered all his forces to take up defensive positions behind the walls. He could at least hope that the forts and ramparts of the city would give him a breathing space in which he could turn the National Guard into a fighting force. What continuously defeated Cluseret was not the army at Versailles, but the National Guard itself. Its inefficiency and indiscipline were notorious. Since all officers of the National Guard were elected, as soon as one of them gave an unpopular order, he could be deposed.

The Commune's military had; no organization, very little clothing, and defective armament. Morale and discipline were at a low point because in every section of the city there were committees and sub-committees that had control of the fighting forces in their area. The Commune's artillery was useless because of their obstinate refusal to go into barracks for mobilization and most of the canons needed No.7 ammunition that was not available until Cluseret found the tools to make it. There was no means of transporting supplies or of scouting because the necessary carriage horses had been stolen, which also meant no cavalry.

Cluseret began the reorganization by working on the Commune's armaments – first, since he had already began manufacturing the canon ammunition, he turned to the mitrailleuses (the rapid firing guns), he chose the American weapon, the Gattling, because of the guns' great range, the fact that they loaded rapidly, and because they were easy to use. As to the reorganization of the infantry, because he had a scarcity of competent officers, Cluseret divided the National Guard into two great divisions, the sedentary and the mobile, and issued the degree which would begin his problems with the Commune – a draft - one however that was only compulsory if one remained in Paris. Even so, Cluseret was criticized because it was believed by

---

184   Gustave Cluseret, *Memoires* I, p. 255

185   Frank Jellinek, *The Paris Commune*, (Hesperides Press, Bel Air, Ca. 2008) p. 199

the leaders of the Commune that this decree dealt a blow to individual liberty. The division of the National Guard forces into sedentary and mobile groups also attacked the idea of 'individual liberty.' The Guardsmen grumbled that the measure 'broke up the bonds of solidarity and fraternity formed during the Siege', but it made sense if any of the National Guard battalions were to be made battle-worthy.[186] This individualism in the National Guard, not the army at Versailles also defeated Cluseret. None of the necessary elements of a fighting force existed in any meaningful way. Conscription only increased the number of disabling illnesses in Paris and it became obvious that committed fighters for the Commune could not be obtained through a draft – the most devoted partisans had been declared too old to serve in the active regiments. The problems also extended into the supply of war material. In the April third attack, many of the Guard had gone into battle short of food and cartridges. As Cluseret remarked, "Never have I seen anything comparable to the anarchy of the National Guard" In addition to his reorganization, he also announced the suppression of the rank of general and the abolition of extravagant uniforms. His circular to the Guard on April seventh declared: …"Forgetting our modest origins, a ridiculous mania for lanyards, gold-braid, rings, and embroidery has begun to appear among us. Workers, you have, for the first time, accomplished the revolution by and for Labour. Let us not deny and above all let us not be ashamed of our origins. Workers we were, workers we are, workers we shall remain."…[187] This call for austerity also did not endear Cluseret to the Parisians.

Even with a victory over the Versailles forces on April ninth, Cluseret could not overcome the obstructionism of the Central Committee of the National Guard. When the Commune ratified Cluseret's appointment, the Central Committee's view of him changed to one of opposition. When Cluseret was elected to the Central Committee of the Commune, the National Guard now stung by his reforms, virtually declared a policy of non-cooperation. On April 16, he set up a Court-Martial and personally arrested a National Guard battalion commander. This action caused the Central Committee to explode with rage at Cluseret, showing their contempt for him by releasing

---

186   Alistair Horne, *The Fall of Paris: The Siege and the Commune,* 1870-71 (Suffolk, England: The Chaucer Press, 1963) p. 383

187   Gustave Cluseret, "The Military Side of the Commune."

the officer a few days later. Undaunted, Cluseret arrested the National Guard officers of the Faubourg St. Germain for refusing to march against the enemy. The power of the Central Committee, spurred on by Cluseret's actions began to manifest itself. First, the decision of the Court Martial was quashed and Cluseret's overruled by the Commune. Next, Cluseret himself came under attack from the Commune for his handling of the defense of Paris, which resulted, on April 23, in a commission of inquiry into the administration of the war.

Although Cluseret was not relieved of his command until April thirtieth, the appointment of this commission was in effect a vote of no confidence in him. The Commune placed the blame for the state of the army on him rather than risk conflict with the true authors of the military debacle, the National Guard. Just before his dismissal, Cluseret attempted to help the Commune in two ways; first, he contacted the German foreign office in an attempt to have the German's mediate the differences between the Commune and the French government – the overture was ignored. Then, although Cluseret had failed to stop the artillery barrage from Mont-Valerien, he did manage to retake Fort Issy, the permanent loss of which would have caused a devastating blow to the defense of Paris.

Issy was saved for the Commune, but by now an irrevocable decision had been taken to replace its military commander. On his return from Issy, he was arrested on charges of "incapacity" on May 1 and held for trial in the prison at Mazas, and accused of corresponding with the Commune's enemies. All things considered, he was lucky to be there, for as Paschal Grousset, a writer and politician explained to the Commune:

> In a revolution - - the Gospel according to Saint Robespierre - - one does not simply recall a War Minister who has lost the confidence of his constituents: one arrests him; and in by-gone days one shot him.[188]

Also, fortunately for Cluseret, the day set for his trial, Sunday, May 21, was also the day that the Versailles forces entered Paris at the start of *la semaine sanglante*.[189] At about 7 p.m. that evening, a member of the Committee of

---

188  Gustave Cluseret, *Memoires*, 2, p. 154-155

189  the bloody week

Public Safety burst into the Hotel de Ville with news of the enemy incursion. As a result, a quick vote was taken by the Commune Council, the outcome was that the charges against Cluseret were dropped by a vote of 28 to 7. Knowing that the game was up, he went into hiding until the bloodletting was over and then escaped from Paris after spending five months disguised as a pious seminarian while hand-to-hand combat raged through the city streets. In the end twenty-five thousand Parisians were killed or summarily shot by the troops from Versailles, who sacked the city while German soldiers and the French bourgeoisie cheered them on. The Commune for its part murdered more than seventy hostages, including the Archbishop and set the city aflame.

On October 29, 1871, Cluseret slipped out of Paris disguised as a Belgian priest. A squad of French soldiers at the Gare du Nord even asked for a blessing, which Cluseret kindly provided; then he boarded his train and left the city.

After escaping from Paris, Cluseret went to ground in a small hotel in Marseilles until November 16. The next day he left France on the steamship *Roi Jerome* en route to Civitavecchia.[190] Cluseret had shaven off his heavy beard and moustaches and now donned the robes of a Dominican friar, as that order was very numerous in France and Italy, especially in Marseilles where they were embarking daily for various parts of Italy. In Rome, Cluseret stayed at the Hotel Delle Isola Brittainche where many prominent members of the Commune congregated before their escapes from Europe, many traveling to the United States. Cluseret however sailed north to England arriving on November 28. At Southampton, he wrote to General La Cecilia[191] who was still in Marseilles:

My Dear Brother: I have at last completely escaped the power of the rulers of the false Republic of Versailles and am free to work with you anew for the regeneration of France. Pardon the brevity of this note. I am too ill and careworn to write you more fully until I arrive in America.

Yours most devotedly[192]

---

190  The port of Rome

191  One of his officers in the Commune

192  "Cluseret's Movements," *New York Times*, December 31, 1871

# 1871-1900

After spending a short time in England, Cluseret journeyed to the United States and then to Switzerland. On August 30, 1872, he was condemned to death *in absentia* by the French government for his actions during the Civil War. In 1876, looking for another opportunity to become involved in combat, this time in Africa where there was tension between England and the Boers, he contacted J.A. Froude,[193]who attempted to secure a military position for him in the government of the Transvaal. The following are excerpts from a series of letters that Froude sent to Cluseret during the years 1876 and 1877.

March 1, 1876

Dear General Cluseret

...I was not unmindful of you when I saw the President of the S A Republic[194]He saw readily the great advantage which he might derive from your presence and assistance[195] *His fear indeed was that your influence might become too great and that you might become a dangerous rival to himself*[196]. Yet he bears you in mind and I shall not be surprised if you hear from him...

    In haste
    Faithfully yours
    J A Froude

---

193  English historian, novelist, biographer, and editor of Fraser's magazine, a journal that Cluseret occasionally wrote articles for.

194  Thomas Francois Burgers

195  Initially, Burgers was interested in Cluseret's services to combat disturbances caused by the Bantu tribe.

196  Froude's italics

March 11, 1876

Dear General Cluseret

…The money which the S A Republic would offer you would be slight. The only adequate reward which so poor a state could offer would be land and permanent office in the Republic. The Dutch farmers are poor themselves. They spend little in their own families and do not understand that one can need more. It is possible that if the President carries out his threat of closing the gold fields there may be fighting there…In that case the President will himself be anxious for your assistance. Let him ask for it himself and you can make your own terms.

Believe me

Sincerely yours

J A Froude


August 11, 1876

Dear General Cluseret

I am sorry that your negotiation with the Transvaal Republic has led to nothing…I wish the President well, and for that reason I should have been glad could he have had such efficient help as yours at his side.

You are no doubt impatient of inactivity[197] but for your own sake I shall be sorry also to hear of your joining the Turks…But you must judge for yourself.

Yours ever-sincerely

J A Froude

---

197  Writing to Lady Derby on September 22, 1876, Froude said he had just received a letter from Cluseret, who had complained, "J'ai la nostalgie de la poudre" (I miss the gunpowder)

November 19, 1876

Dear General Cluseret

…You will be fighting against fate if you take service under the Porte.[198]If the present ministry attempt to bring us into war with Russia they will be out of office in 6 months and Mr. Gladstone will come back and bring with him a Russian alliance. I am confident that I tell you the truth.

Faithfully yours

J A Froude


January 24, 1877

Dear General Cluseret

I have left your long letter unanswered. I made enquiries in your behalf, and waited till I had something definite to say. I could do little with the English journals, but there appears to be a chance with the New York Herald or the New York Tribune.

I have seen the editor of the Herald (or one of his principal managers of it) and have strongly recommended you. I understand from him that he has been in communication with you. Failing this my American friends mean to apply to the Tribune and I hope have already do so.[199]…

Ever sincerely yours

J A Froude

---

198  The former Ottoman court or the government in Turkey.

199  Finding employment for Cluseret

March 2, 1877

Dear General Cluseret

...I cannot speak with certainty, but I believe that the time is passed when you could have been of use in the Transvaal. Had the President accepted your services when I recommended him to employ you the Republic would now have been triumphant and secure of independence...if the President had accepted your help the Republic would have been able to enter the Union on more favourable terms. But it is now too late. I would not wish to see you go there, for you would have no field open to you in which to distinguish yourself.

Yours truly,

J A Froude[200]


Later in 1877, Cluseret did join the Turkish military in its war with Russia. After the war, he remained in Turkey reuniting with a Civil War friend, Horace Maynard, who was now the American minister there. Since Cluseret was, as usual, low on funds, Maynard gave him a collection of materials for a report on Turkish cereals for the Agricultural Department in Washington. However, before the report was completed, Maynard resigned

After France declared an amnesty in 1881 Cluseret returned to Paris and began contributing to the newspapers *La Commune* and *La Marseillaise*. His articles, which attempted to incite the French army to insubordination caused his arrest and imprisonment for two years and additionally, he paid a fine of 3000 francs.

In 1885, the new Turkish ambassador, Samuel S. "Sunset" Cox arrived in Constantinople, purchased some pictures that Cluseret had painted,[201]listened to his claim for compensation, and, when the Turkish mission was abandoned in 1886 and he was re-elected to Congress, succeeded in securing an appropriation from the lower house on Cluseret's behalf. Not

---

200  "Letters of James Anthony Froude," Edited by Raymond M. Bennett, *The Journal of the Rutgers University Library*, Vol. 1, Issue 1, 1961, p. 10-23

201  Cluseret was also an accomplished artist.

long afterwards, Senator William M. Evarts of New York submitted the same bill, which was passed in 1888, allowing Cluseret to obtain his money by applying to the United States Legation in Paris.

This money, which amounted to five hundred dollars, completely paid his election expenses when Cluseret entered the final phase of his remarkable career, that of politician. He stood for election to the Chamber of Deputies from the city of Toulon. Although he won, the moderate members of the Chamber challenged his election, not wanting a former member of the Commune, who had been condemned to death *in contumaciam,*[202] and who had been recently amnestied, take his seat. The argument used to attempt to invalidate his election was based on the fact that Cluseret was an American citizen. Cluseret had never denied that he was a citizen of the United States, and more than that affirmed it with evident pleasure up to the very day of his death. Fortunately for Cluseret, when the Chamber consulted the highest French legal authorities, they declared that he had not lost his French citizenship and was therefore allowed to enter the Chamber. Cluseret was re-elected several times and was a member of the Chamber of Deputies when he died near Hyeres, Department of the Var, August 22, 1900.[203]

---

202  In contempt of court

203  Theodore Stanton, "Gen. Cluseret as an American," *The Nation,* August 15, 1901, p. 129-130

# Epilogue

Gustave Cluseret was an individual comprised of three factors; a military background, ambition, and a search for a political philosophy. While his military ability and ambition would remain steadfast throughout his life, his political ideals changed through time.

Born in Paris in June 1823, he was the son and grandson of military officers. In 1841 he entered the military academy of St. Cyr, He saw combat soon after graduation in the Paris uprising of June 1848 fighting on the side of the bourgeois moderates, earning the Legion of Honor while smashing the workers barricades. But this youthful act was not a true harbinger of Cluseret's future political development, for within a year he was relieved from duty for openly criticizing President Louis Napoleon.[204]

Cluseret swallowed his political misgivings long enough to rejoin the French Army in the mid 1850's serving with distinction in Algeria and the Crimea. By 1858, however he became permanently estranged from the Empire and left the army for good, crossing the Atlantic and landing a job at a New York bank. In 1860, he re-crossed the Atlantic to fight with Garibaldi for Italian liberation. It was in Italy in September 1861 that the Frenchman heard about Secretary of State William Seward's appeal to European military officers.

During the next ten years, Cluseret would become involved in two civil wars and a rising in three different countries, in which his anchor, his military skill would come to the fore and hold him in good stead, unfortunately skill's other component, luck did not.

As an officer in the Union Army, Cluseret only fought in one engagement – at the Battle of Cross Keys, serving with distinction, and earning a promotion to General for his "skill and gallantry" (in General Fremont's opinion). This

---

204   Ella Lonn, Foreigners in the Union Army and Navy, p. 273-275

was to be the end of his American military career since he alienated his superiors and reinforced his reputation as a troublemaker.[205]Because of his only one success in battle, he believed that his American experience was a flop. In a rare burst of candor, he even confessed to Charles Sumner "I am a loser"[206]

In the United States, Cluseret could not follow up on his success, in Ireland, he never reached the point of actually fighting, but his military background prevented him from becoming involved in an unsuccessful endeavor, that of attempting to fight with too few troops. Also, his plan of guerilla warfare was probably the correct strategy, since the massed attack against The English forces failed under another commander.

Finally, there was his experience in the Commune. Unlike the Union Army in which he commanded professional troops, here he had to make do with a ragtag collection of would-be soldiers and officers, combined with a complete lack of discipline, few supplies, and a lack of support from his superiors. Even so, he managed to create a credible fighting force before being arrested and thus avoided being killed or captured by the advancing French Army.

For most people, a cycle of failures like this would lead to utter despair. But for Cluseret, like many other committed believers, personal failure (although in these instances involving bad luck) only intensified his commitment to external ideals.[207]

Cluseret's politics were obviously mutable, and contemporaries attributed the changes to crass ambition. Karl Marx, for one, called the Frenchman a "lousy, importunate, vain, and over-ambitious babbler."[208]The *New York Times* added that Cluseret "has no positive principle, being regulated, so far

---

205  Years later, the *New York Times* called him an "irrepressible grumbler," November 27, 1888

206  Cluseret to Sumner, September 22, 1864

207  Gustave Cluseret, "My Connection with Fenianism," *Fraser's Magazine*, n.s., 2 (1872) p. 31-46

208  Marx to Frederick Engels, *Marx and Engels Collected Works*, (London: 1975) Vol. 44, p. 70

as he is regulated at all, by vanity and self interest."[209]Yet a good deal of the abuse is unwarranted. On occasion his principles did indeed wander, but this did not make him a mere adventurer, "adopt [ing] whatever principles…his sword upheld."[210]

The causes that Cluseret upheld were consistently progressive, and he was shaped by their principles much more than he knew. At no time was this more evident than during the 1860s. At the start of the American Civil War, Cluseret was a bourgeois army officer with republican leanings and an uncertain record of counter-revolution.[211]His most important literary effort to date had been a pamphlet on military reform addressed to the king of Italy. A decade late Cluseret had become a committed social revolutionary; his writings had appeared in a half-dozen left-wing journals and his republican friends of the 1860s both French and American had been abandoned as too conservative.[212]The cause? Cluseret had been radicalized by his immersion in American political culture.[213]As far as his ambition was concerned, as he himself wrote, "who is not?"[214]

---

209  The *New York Times*, January 30, 1880

210  Edmond Lepelletier, Histoire de la Commune de 1871, 3 Vols. (Paris: 1911-1913), Vol. 3, p. 194. Cluseret's obituarist in the *New York Herald* strongly disagreed, writing that "The Frenchman's love of an idea animated him, and its pursuit led him [onward]" (August 24, 1900).

211  Cluseret to Sumner, April 30 and August 19, 1862, and April 16,1865

212  Gustave Cluseret, Memoires, Vol. 2, p. 267

213  Philip M. Katz, *From Appomattox to Montmartre, Americans and the Paris Commune*, (Cambridge: Harvard University Press, 1998) p. 6

214  Unsigned article by Cluseret in the *Army and Navy Journal*, May 6, 1865, p. 579

# Bibliography – Books

Blight, David W. and Brooks D. Simpson, eds. *Union and Emancipation Essays on Politics and Race in the Civil War Era*. Kent, Ohio: Kent State University Press, 1997

Cox, Jacob D. *Military Reminiscences of the Civil War*, Volume 1, April 1861-November 1863. New York: Charles Scribner's Sons, 1900

Cluseret, Gustave P. *Armee et democratie*. Paris< 1869

Cluseret, Gustave P. *Memories*. Paris, 1887

Cluseret, Gustave P. *Mexico and the Solidarity of Nations*. Reprint, Whitefish, Montana. Kessinger Publishing LLC, 2012

Evans, Howard. *Sir Randal Cremer*. London: Fisher Uwin, 1909

Hendrick, Burton J. *Lincoln's War Cabinet*. Boston: Literary Licensing, LLC, 2012

Horne, Alistair. The Fall of Paris: *The Siege and the Commune, 1870-1871*. Suffolk, England: The Chaucer Press, 1963

Jackson, T. A. *Ireland, Her Own*. New York: Lawrence and Wishart, 1971

Jellinek, Frank. *The Paris Commune*. Bel-Air, California: Hesperides Press, 2008

Katz, Philip M. *From Appomattox to Montmartre*. Cambridge: Harvard University Press, 1998

Land, Theodore F. *Loyal West Virginia, From 1861 to 1865*. Baltimore,

Maryland: The Deutsch Publishing Co., 1865

Le Caron, Major Henri, *Twenty-Five Years in the Secret Service. The Recollections of a Spy*. London: Forgotten Books, 2012

Leno, John Bedford. *The Aftermath*. London: Reeves and Turner, 1892

Lepell, Edmond. *Historie de la Commune de 1871,* 3 Vols. Paris, 1911-1913, Vol.3 p. 194

Lonn, Ella. *Foreigners in the Union Army and Navy.* Baton Rouge Louisiana: Louisiana State University Press, 1951

McClellan, George B. *McClellan's Own Story: The War for the Union. The Soldiers Who Fought It. The Civilians who Directed It, and his Relations to It and to Them.* New York: Charles Webster and Company, 1887

McDonald, Cornelia. *A Diary: with Reminiscences of the War and Refugee Life in the Shenandoah Valley,* 1860-1865. Louisville: Collom and Ghertner, 1935

McPherson, Edward. *The Political History of the United States of America During the Great Rebellion* (2nd Edition) Washington: Andesite Press, 2015

Moore, Frank. *The Rebellion Record: A Diary of American Events, With Documents, Narratives, Illustrative Incidents, Poetry, Etc.* New York: G. P. Putnam, 1868

Nevins, Allan. Fremont, *Pathfinder of the West* (3rd Edition) Lincoln: University of Nebraska Press. 1992

Newsinger, John. *Fenianism in Mid-Victorian* Britain. London: Pluto Press, 1994

Novalas, Johnathon A. *My Will is Absolute Law: A Biography of Union General Robert H. Milroy.* Jefferson, North Carolina: McFarland and Company, Publisher, 2006

Rutherford, John. *The Secret History of the Fenian Conspiracy, Its Origins. Objects, and Ramifications*, Vol. LL. London: C. Kegan Paul and Co.,

1877

Sears, Stephen W. *The Civil War Papers of George B. McClellan: Selected Correspondence,* 1860-1865. Cambridge: Da Capo Press, 1992

Thornton, Willis. *The Nine Lives of Citizen Train.* New York: Greenberg Publishing, 1948

Train, George Francis. *My Life in Many States and in Foreign Lands.* New York: D. Appleton and Company, 1902

Tweed, William M. in "Dictionary of American Biography, ed. Dumas Malone. New York: 1936, XIX

Washburne, Elihu B. *Reflections of a Minister to France,* 1869-1877. New York: C. Scribner's Sons, 1887


**Articles and Dissertation**

"General Cluseret's Dossier," London Daily Telegraph, April 24, 1871

"Letters of James Anthony Froude," Edited by Raymond M. Bennett. *The Journal of the Rutgers University Library*, Vol. 1, Issue 1, 1961

Blaisdell, Lowell I. "A French Civil War Adventurer: Fact and Fancy," *Civil War History*, Vol. XIII, September, 1966, No. 111

Blaisdell, Lowell, I. "Cluseret and the Freemont Campaign of 1864," *Mid America*, October 1964, Vol. 46, No. 4

Cluseret, Gustave P. "My Connection With Fenianism," *Littell's Living Age.* No. 114, 1873

Cluseret, Gustave P. "The Military Side of the Commune." *The Fortnightly Review*, No. LXXIX, New Series, July 1, 1873

Katz, Mark Philip. "Americanizing the Paris Commune, 1861 -1868. PhD dissertation, Princeton University, January 1994

Kennedy, Padraic. "The Secret Service Department: A British Intelligence

Bureau in Mid-Victorian London, September 1867 to April 1868." *Intelligence and National Security*, Vol. 18, No. 3 (autumn, 2003)

Newsinger, John. "A Great Blow Must be Struck in Ireland: Karl Marx and the Fenians." *Race and Class,* 1982, 24:151

Simpson, Brook D. "Lincoln and his Political Generals," Journal of the Abraham Lincoln Association, Vol. 21, No. 1, Winter 2000

**Newspapers Consulted**

New York Times

New Nation

London Times

The New York World

Evening Post

# Index

# V

# W